# The Extreme Novelist

The No-Time-to-Write Method for Drafting
Your Novel in 8 Weeks

Kathryn Johnson

KATHRYN JOHNSON

For additional information regarding
this book or to contact the author
for speaking engagements:
Kathryn@WriteByYou.com

Cover Art by Earthly Charms

## Table of Contents

### Chapters

KATHRYN JOHNSON

Acknowledgments:

Many people helped transform *The Extreme Novelist* course into a book.

Out of that generous crowd, special appreciation goes to my talented editor, Barb Goffman. Also to my beta readers—Irene Vartanoff, Eugenia Sozzi, Jo Donaldson, and Kerry Peresta—for their insight and wise suggestions.

In addition, the Columbia Writers' Critique Group inspired and supported this author throughout the project.

Finally, my wonderful students at The Writer's Center, gifted writers in their own right, deserve a huge thank you. They've taught me at least as much as I have taught them.

## Chapter 1: What's So Extreme About Writing a Novel?

Everything!

If you've tried writing fiction of any length—short stories, novellas, a novel—you know it's not easy. Yes, writing stories can be fun. Letting the imagination run free, creating rich and memorable characters, and then spinning an amazing tale around them. Fantastic! But if we're to attract readers who find value in our fiction and will return to read us whenever we publish new work, we must invest thought and hard work in our literary projects.

Students in my novel-writing classes at *The Writer's Center* accept the need to focus on and devote effort to their books. If they complain at all about the process, they mention two issues. The first is finding the time to write. The second is facing the daunting task of writing so many words. (In today's publishing world 70–80,000 words, on average, for an adult novel.)

You may be all too familiar with the time issue. Have you labored over drafting a book for many months? (Years?) Then you know that writing gobbles up hours. Who in the twenty-first century has spare time on their hands? Most adults must hold onto their day job, whatever that may be, to pay for basic necessities—housing, food, clothing, and transportation. Many of us also support a partner and/or children, possibly even parents, grandparents, or grandchildren.

We can't risk walking away from a steady income in the hope of selling a book that will take the place of our current income. (It would need to be a wildly successful one at that!) Thus, we need to find ways to write while maintaining our day job and other responsibilities.

Easier said than done?

Just thinking about writing book-length fiction can be overwhelming—if only in terms of the magnitude of the project. We can easily become intimidated. Perhaps even terrified that we're doomed to failure!

Is there a solution to these dilemmas? How do we put aside enough time and energy to write eighty thousand (or so) words when our lives are already so busy—*and* sustain our focus and courage long enough to do so? One answer is: We become Extreme Novelists by making our writing a priority.

"How?" you ask. Keep on reading; I'll show you.

But first, I want to assure you of one important thing: I know you can do this. I know that no matter how busy or complicated your life is, you can accomplish your goal of writing a novel. I know this because, time and again, I've seen my students transform their frustrated-writer lives into a satisfying routine of daily writing, dedicated to their love of fiction. You will learn specific methods. You will choose from among them those that work most effectively for you. You will get the job done.

I, too, have a personal goal. It is, simply put, to give you the writing life you desire and deserve.

### *Is Becoming an Extreme Novelist for You?*

Before diving into the program in earnest, let's take a moment to see if we're a good match.

Do you sometimes find yourself saying to family members, friends, or an author acquaintance, "I would love to write a book someday, but I just can't seem to find the time."

Do you collect interesting characters, settings, and plot ideas for stories and launch into writing an opening chapter or two with enthusiasm—only to lose momentum and give up in frustration before completing a single story?

Have you attempted to closet yourself away from distractions in order to write—but found it hopeless?

Or perhaps you sense that you've alienated people close to you by seeking private time for your beloved writing.

Have you been working on the same story for five, ten, fifteen years or more?

If any of these situations sound familiar, I believe the Extreme Novelist program will work for you. I can say this because I've walked in your shoes.

When I first started working toward a writing career, I was accused of being "selfish" by my then-partner. "You're neglecting

6

me and the children," I was told. Was I? I didn't think so. I was still the person who cleaned the house, did the family's laundry, drove the kids to school, shopped for groceries, and cooked everyone's meals. I also worked at a full-time job outside of the home. But because I "stole" an hour or two out of my days to write, I was being selfish. Does this sound at all familiar?

Over and over again I hear similar stories from authors, both women and men, who attend my classes or hear me speak at writers' conferences. People who have never experienced the joy of creating stories are unable to understand the appeal of the writing process— and often view it as a threat to the relationship. Something akin to taking a lover. (Without the physical pleasure.)

Many would-be authors are discouraged in other ways. Exhaustion plays a huge role in parting us from our dreams of publication. When we work one or more jobs, and possibly suffer through demanding commutes, as many do in the Washington, DC, area where I live, it sometimes seems there's nothing left of us with which to focus on writing.

There's no time. No energy. No ability to concentrate our weary, stressed brains on a story, or even find the inspiration to write— regardless of how much we may *want* to. We are so involved in our complex, demanding world that we sometimes feel trapped by the life we signed on for—willingly or not—years ago. We can see no route to having the writerly life of our dreams. We're stuck.

And that is incredibly sad.

We wish to escape the gray sameness of our lives. To retreat to that idyllic cabin in the woods and blissful isolation, where we can dedicate ourselves to writing our books. But there seems little hope of that dream ever becoming a reality. Even if we love our day job (and of course would never think of deserting our family), the lure of authorship taunts us. We just want the chance to see if we can *do* it. Can we become published, share our stories with the world, maybe even fashion a new lifestyle and livelihood out of writing?

And so we continue to wonder: *Even if by some miracle I'm released from my work and family obligations, will the effort be worth it?* In short, how can I, as a novice fiction writer, know that the resulting manuscript will be good enough to interest readers?

This book is for writers who are willing to take the leap of faith that all authors take when they sit down to craft words into a story. I suspect, since you've read this far, this means *you*. You will learn how to *make time for your craft* while still functioning in the real world, if that's what you honestly want.

But let's be clear. This isn't the same thing as *finding the time* to write. The months required to write a novel will never jump up and offer themselves to you. We're talking about literally *creating time* for our writing—and that's entirely different.

Ready to take the plunge? Read on.

### *Make Time for Your Writing*

To build time for writing into your life, you will make some subtle (or, if necessary, major) changes in your daily routine. That means giving up a few activities you've become accustomed to and, possibly, rearranging your daily schedule.

Because habits are hard to break, these changes will mean a mental adjustment on your part. But you may be surprised by how little you miss the one or two cast-off chores and time-wasters that have wormed their way into your life.

If you're anything like my wonderful students, you'll be amazed by how gratifying this new way of living your life as a working writer can be. Follow the tips and suggestions throughout this book, trying out new ones even if you're at first a little skeptical about them working. Experiment with your own versions of what has benefitted others. You'll learn which practices work best for you. Within a few weeks you will have discovered practical, effective ways to give your writing the priority status it deserves.

As you follow the simple logic of this program, the pages of your draft will accumulate quickly and consistently, day by day. That's a good thing, of course. Because the goal in becoming an Extreme Novelist is to develop a full rough draft of your novel in 8–10 weeks.

A rapid first draft, completed within approximately two months, defines the shape and establishes the structure for your novel. It also goes a long way toward reassuring you, the writer, that you are capable of achieving your goal of actually completing a book. And every day that you write in this aggressive, rapidly paced manner, your confidence as a fiction author will increase.

I tell my students that this course is challenging, exciting, a little scary, too. I also warn them that they may never write the same way again. Hopefully, that's a good thing. But at the very least, the new habits you establish will give you a different and focused way of tackling the writing of your long fiction.

*A few words of caution:* This first draft won't be pretty. We refer to it as *rough* for a reason. Don't count on showing the resulting pages to a literary agent or publisher, or even to a pre-publication editor. It won't be ready for other eyes. (Think: James Bond. "For Your Eyes Only.") The flowing, perfectly honed prose that you aspire to comes later. A complete story draft—beginning, middle, and end—told through active, vivid scenes, is a necessary early step toward the finished product you envision. And that product will be a book with your name, as the author, on its cover.

In addition to all of the above-mentioned benefits, you'll learn to write aggressively and with a professional attitude, not just when you feel "inspired." This workmanlike approach will carry you through the revision process as well. It's then that you'll search for perfect words, and polish each and every sentence.

Furthermore, if you are of a mind to see your work published, these same professional skills will support you through the process of submitting your novels to, and interacting with, literary agents and acquiring editors of publishing houses. Or you may choose to become your own publisher. No single choice is for everyone. Ultimately, the form your novel takes will be up to you.

I believe that if you wish to write a novel—even if you've never written short stories, poems, or anything other than business letters, technical papers, or those newsy notes sent to friends and family on the holidays—*you can learn!* Writing fiction isn't a talent one is born with; it's a learnable skill.

How can I make such an outrageous statement with such confidence?

I've seen my students do it, time and again. This is because they, *and you*, have what all human beings possess: the *Storytelling Gene.* It is, in fact, one of our most basic, innate survival skills.

# KATHRYN JOHNSON

### *The Storyteller as Survivor*

We human beings are instinctively programmed to teach, learn, and entertain through stories. This process begins in the very earliest moments of our lives, as we absorb the concept of language. The adults in our lives—the smart ones, that is—warn us of danger by telling us stories of what will happen if we ignore basic safety rules.

"Do you see this scar on my arm? That's where I touched the hot stove when I was about your age, and I burned myself. It really hurt." This is far more effective than shaking a finger at a child, scolding, or rattling off a list of household rules. Stories make warnings vivid, real, something the listener can identify with—whereas shouting and lectures are often ignored. Stories are fun!

It works the same way for adults. Our ancestors undoubtedly warned each other not to venture into a specific cave after having seen a bear enter it. Sailors told of sea monsters and ships that sailed off the ends of the earth to steer their mates away from treacherous waters. Every religion uses stories to teach its beliefs.

True stories and fantasies are equally irresistible, whether told around a campfire, read from a picture book at bedtime, or enjoyed digitally on a tablet. Our culture has become visually hooked by stories in movies, videos, and TV shows. If you are the kind of person who likes to escape into a rich and compelling tale for hours or even days at a time—either by reading or creating stories—then you may well be a born novelist.

I've been writing novels for a very long time. At the time of my revising this chapter, over forty of my novels have been published by major publishers. I continue to seek publication with what we now think of as the "Big Five" in American publishing: Hachette, HarperCollins, Macmillan, Penguin Random House, and Simon & Schuster.

I'm also working with a small press on some projects, because they are sometimes more open to new ideas. Over the years I've picked up a good deal of practical experience in the planning, writing, and production of books. So these days I'm also experimenting with self-publishing (aka indie publishing). Through this third method of publication I can reach even more readers, many of whom enjoy the sorts of stories that commercial presses aren't willing to get behind enthusiastically.

### *Where Did the Extreme Novelist Come From?*

Seven years ago I started teaching at a nonprofit school located inside the Washington, DC, beltway, whose mission was (and is) to provide a comprehensive program of adult writing programs. I was asked to develop a course to be called: *Writing the Popular Novel*. It included tips on developing plots and characters for a variety of genres: Mystery, Romance, Science Fiction, Action-Adventure, Women's Fiction, Suspense, and so forth. Just as we had hoped, the course attracted a wide range of students interested in working in their favorite genres.

But the real challenge for me as a teacher was not the subject matter. It was the students themselves—or more to the point, it was the reasons my students gave for not having been able to complete their books.

They ranged in age from eighteen and into their eighties. Most were (or had been) professional men and women employed in a variety of highly competitive, sophisticated, stressful, and demanding occupations. Lawyers, doctors, speech writers, graphic artists, journalists, teachers, business owners, international bankers—the list goes on. Frankly, their worldly experiences, mastery of the English language, and desire to write convinced me that there was no reason they shouldn't have already completed their long-dreamt-of novels and found a publisher. But every single one of them was frustrated, having failed at their efforts. They seemed incapable of prying writing time out of their already busy weeks and overwhelmed by the sheer enormity of the task of writing a book.

They told me:

"There isn't even a half hour to spare for writing in my crazy-busy days."

"Constant interruptions and things I must do to keep up with my day job get in the way of my writing. Then there are my family responsibilities."

"I write a chapter or two then lose the inspiration and become disheartened with my ideas."

"I can't come up with a *good enough* concept. Nothing at all original."

"I write on a computer all day at work. It's hard to come home at the end of a long day and then type even more when I'm feeling so wasted."

The two common factors they shared, as novelists, were a perceived lack of time to write and fragile self-confidence. Some voiced the dream of quitting their day job and becoming a full-time writer. The sooner the better. They just didn't know how to go about making the writing happen.

### *Find Out What's Stopping You*

What struck me as most interesting was this: Every one of these people could already write quite well. They, much like you, I'd guess, had been doing it all of their lives. They possessed the necessary basic tools: the ability to understand grammar, to spell correctly, to write a sentence and compose readable paragraphs. With a little guidance to augment their business and personal writing competence with fiction skills, they should have been able to at least get their books into draft form.

Not so! Many had been taking courses for years or struggling along on their own. Trying again and again, and failing for five years or even five decades! *Why?* I asked myself. This just didn't make sense to me. I'd been writing, on average, two novels a year for a couple of decades. And I'll be the first to admit that I'm neither a genius nor unusually gifted.

I started paying even closer attention to the composition of my classes. Each semester that I taught the course, my classroom was chock-full of bright, eager faces and intelligent minds. Some students were already retired and admitted they should have plenty of time to write—but their lives seemed as busy as ever. Each had honestly tried to write the book that had bloomed in their head. Some managed to complete a few short stories, some poetry, or they had banged out two or three chapters before giving up on their novel.

They'd come to my class looking for an answer to the question: *Why can't I do this? Why can't I, a reasonably intelligent and educated person, write a publishable novel?*

That started me thinking about a different sort of course. One for adults who needed structure and practical guidance that would help them through the challenging process of getting a book written.

To my way of thinking, it shouldn't matter what a person's current career situation, age, sex, social life, religion, ethnic, or educational background happens to be. All my students need, I reasoned, is a working knowledge of the language in which they propose to publish, and a few basic fiction skills. That includes an understanding of how to create scenes, string them together into chapters, and from these grow a book-length story. As long as they allow their imaginations the freedom to create, and are willing to learn from the authors they love to read, they *should* be able to craft novels for their own pleasure and the enjoyment of others.

But the first step—as they themselves told me—was snagging the time and confidence to get a full draft of their book written. And to do that I knew they needed to make some dramatic changes in their lives and establish new habits. They had to move from the realm of the hobbyist author, who writes only when inspired and well rested and time is easily available—into the gritty working world of the pro. They also needed to break free from their fear of failure, and gain trust in their own abilities and the exciting possibility of publication.

This was the beginning of *The Extreme Novelist*, a down-to-earth, common-sense approach that anyone can use to write their novel. If you enjoy and are helped by this book—it is, in no small part, thanks to my amazing students. For they are the ones who inspired *me* by asking, "Why don't you put this course in a book?"

### *Eliminate Barriers*

First we need to talk about what this book is *not*. It isn't one of those slick, gimmicky writing models that demand you stuff your story into a pre-designed plot pattern or follow someone else's ideas of what you can or can't do in your story.

Neither is this book intended to teach you *how* to write fiction. Zillions of pages and entire books (libraries!) have been written on the topics of Plotting, Characterization, Perspective, and fitting one's stories into specific genres.

Rather, *The Extreme Novelist* is meant to provide methods and inspiration to help you work effectively, in a partnership with your basic knowledge of fiction writing. Furthermore, since you've decided to tackle the mother of all fiction projects—The Novel—I assume you've taken a class or two on writing fiction, done a little reading on the subject, or experimented on your own for a while.

Now that you've done that much and you're still struggling to spit out a story, it's time to eliminate the barriers standing in your way. This book is all about getting the job done. (You may have already figured that out!)

Some tips will work better for you than others. There are no rules, only suggestions that are time-tested by other writers. And pul-lease, don't try to con yourself by saying, "Oh, well, sure—a full-time writer can manage a couple of novels a year. She doesn't have all the distractions and responsibilities I have. She doesn't have a day job."

The truth of the matter is, only the very smallest percentage of writers who consider themselves professional novelists support themselves and their families solely on the income from their novels. They almost always have full-time jobs in addition to the time they spend writing, just as they have families to care for, community and religious obligations, and financial and health concerns. In short, they are just like the rest of us. The difference is, they have learned to put their writing first, at least for the time it takes to get a book written.

It means that out of each day, the one thing they make certain they do is *plan and execute their writing time*. The alternative is just too grim to consider. Writers write. It's in our blood. Once we stop doing it consistently, we eventually just...stop. And that can darn near kill you, or at least make you a pretty miserable person.

The good news is, once we realize the reason we haven't been able to get our books written, we can agree that something has to give. Something has to change. And the change that's going to happen is, I repeat, *YOU!* You are going to learn how to "live in the book." You are going to give a hunk of your life to your writing, and I'll be here to help you do it.

Why should you do anything that sounds do drastic?

Because it's all about *you*, my friend. Face it. Isn't this what you've wanted for a long time? Haven't you longed to have a writer's life, to spin your stories and know that others are reading and enjoying them? Your life may suck (or it may be great), but something's missing. It's okay to feel dissatisfied and want different, more fulfilling days.

In fact, it's more than just okay because, when you think about it, isn't nearly everything that you do about something, or someone, other than you? You work for a company, business, partnership, or the government. You take care of your partner, spouse, children, and others who are dear to you, as best you can. You volunteer for community projects, make time for school or civic meetings, and basically do for everyone else.

Your creative writing is different. It's personal, intimate. It's *yours*. No one will ever order you to write a novel, or fire you if you don't. It's a choice. This is all about your creativity, what you envision and wish to share with others through a great story.

So let's not feel frustrated one more day. Let's. Just. Do it.

## Chapter 2: I Want to Write a Novel. Where Do I Start?

***Silence "The Voices"***

Do I need to explain what these voices are and where they come from? You've heard them, I know you have. The Voices are why we fail to get the book in our head down on paper. They are the reason why, even if we ride our wave of inspiration through drafting the first two, three, or more chapters of our novel, we run into an impenetrable wall of self-doubt. Sometimes we label that wall *Writer's Block*. Other times we just collapse in despair and decide that we aren't good enough writers to pull off this novel-writing gig.

The Voices are always negative, accusatory, slamming us at our most vulnerable moments. They may be internal, coming to us from deep within our soul:

*"No one will ever want to read what I write. Face it—I'm nobody. Only famous or really smart people get publishing contracts."*

*"Everything I write is crap."*

Or they may be external, delivered by the mouths of our closest friends and family members:

*"There are already too many books in the world. How will readers even find yours in the crowd?"*

*"Aren't you a little too old to start a new career?"*

The Voices are most damaging when the internal and external voices echo each other. The apparent logic behind their discouraging harangues becomes almost impossible for the writer to ignore.

***But I'm No Genius!***

When I first entertained the possibility of writing fiction for a living, I was a military wife living in a foreign country with my infant daughter and husband. I loved to read and devoured novels written by Isaac Asimov, Kenneth Roberts, Agatha Christie, Georges Simenon, and Arthur Conan Doyle. If the possibility occurred to me to write any kind of fiction, I sternly reminded myself that these authors were obviously geniuses. I was not intellectually in the same class. Not by a long shot.

But invariably, another idea followed on the tail of this admonition: *There have been millions of books written by thousands upon thousands of authors the world over. How can every one of them have been a genius?*

Logically, the answer is: *That's unlikely, isn't it? Not everyone who writes can be brilliant.* In fact, I'd read books that I thought weren't all that good. If these lesser mortals could turn out a novel that merited shelf space in the military base library I frequented, and presumably elsewhere in the world, didn't it make sense that I also might be capable of writing a passable book?

I started writing.

I would need another twelve years before my first novel was published. I plugged away at one story after another, learning my craft, ignoring my own insecurities as best I could. I shut out the negative voices from others who thought I was being foolish. Or worse, who scolded me for being selfish with my time and dreams. I repeated a mantra to keep me going: *If they can do it, so can I!* My innate stubbornness helped, too.

### Shut Down The Voices

*Internal Negative Messages* intimidate us and keep us from our dream of writing. If we listen to them, we have sealed our own fate. We are acquiescing to failure. The Voices get louder and louder, more and more insistent. They whisper, and threaten, and warn us over and over again that the sensible thing to do is to give up. Just quit. Do something else that's easier or delivers results faster...or just numbs the mind. (Like watching another TV sitcom.)

*External Negative Messages* reinforce our sense of helplessness and despair. Each time someone voices doubt about our writing endeavors, we lose a little hope. It doesn't even require hurtful words. All this person we respect needs to do is respond with a skeptical look to our proud announcement that we're writing a novel.

Even though they may wish us luck, their underlying message reaches us. They disapprove of what we're trying to do. They may say they're concerned for our welfare and simply don't want to see us disappointed. No doubt some naysayers truly worry on our behalf.

But it's not their job to choose how we spend our time or in what dream we invest our heart.

As writers we must be prepared for ostensibly well-meaning advice. Unfortunately, jealousy often has more to do with these warnings of disaster than anxiety over another person's future. After all, you are actually *doing* something they might have never imagined attempting, even if the quiet wish is there. (*I'd love to be able to write for a living!*) How will they feel if you succeed, but they never even tried? You are the brave one, perhaps the person they wish they could be. You are the one who, through your efforts to write, reminds them that they are less daring.

It's vital that we learn to ignore the voices promising doom and failure—whether in our minds or from elsewhere. One way to combat these negative messages is by writing a very fast first draft. By writing swiftly, we allow ourselves to become so absorbed in the process we don't have spare brain cells to pay attention to the evil imp inside us or the naysayers in our world.

We become so caught up in the process of making a book that we simply can't be bothered with anything else—except maybe clocking in at the day job, catching up on a little family news, or throwing in a load of laundry between dashing off exciting scenes. Writing becomes a priority, something we would no more forget to do each day than eating.

Later in this book, we'll look at many ways Extreme Novelists have found to silence The Voices—internal and external. For now, what we need is a plan. We need to restructure our lives in a way that will allow us time to write. That means setting priorities, because if we continue in our old routine (which is already crammed to overflowing with things we must, must, *must* do) we will never *find* the time to write. In fact, let me state this one more time: ***You will never find time to write!***

But you can *make* time to write. There's a huge difference.

How do you make the time to write? You will determine, based on your unique lifestyle and the most important elements in your world—family, work, religion, hobbies, other responsibilities—a writing program that will suit the individual that you are. This program is going to change some of your daily habits and restructure your days to enable you to do the writing that you long to do.

I've witnessed these changes work time and again for hundreds of writers. If you follow in their wake, within 8–10 weeks you will have created a compelling story (in rough form) and established a satisfying writing life for yourself. You'll be well on your way to completing a publishable novel. And, if you wish, you then will have the tools necessary to continue writing and producing one or more books a year, as good if not better than novels written and sold by other professional writers.

So, now that we've identified those negative voices, we know them for what they are—disruptive nonsense or pure maliciousness that must be ignored. Let's take the next step to making that happen.

### *Make a Plan*

How much, when, and where we write depends solely upon the individual writer. In my *Extreme Novelist* classes every student signs a contract promising me, their classmates, and themselves to adhere to certain "rules of the road." We accept that we are accountable for our time. There are few legitimate excuses for not writing.

Rather than showing you the original version of the contract that my students receive a week before the first day of class, we're providing a modified version more suited to writers who live at a distance from the Washington, DC, area and can't physically be in the classroom with me.

### The Extreme Novelist's Rules

*1)* Participating authors agree to an intense personal writing schedule of at least ninety minutes each day, six days a week. *When* you choose to write each day is up to you, but you must *make* and *protect* that time. If you miss a writing day, you will make up that time later in the week. If you are traveling, you will still dedicate writing time during those days. *We are creating writing muscle and building strong writing habits.*

*2)* Our goal is to produce pages. Period. Although, ultimately, we all hope to deliver quality prose to acquiring book editors, and readers, our immediate job is to move closer to a completed rough draft of a novel. Therefore, we will use "automatic writing," releasing ourselves from the urge to edit or criticize our own words. Emphasis will be on scene building, including action, dialogue, plot development, and emotion. Narration will be the glue that binds the story, but not the sole tool.

3) All students must come to their writing time (and place, wherever that may be) prepared to *write*. That may mean carrying a laptop computer (with fully charged battery, in case outlets aren't available), or having paper and pen/pencil handy. Plot outlines, research material, and other notes on hand will mean less wasted time.

4) *No Screen Staring!* If you feel unable to move forward with your current or next scene, write anywhere else in the story. *Do not stop typing until the end of your session!* By continuing to move your hands, you'll keep your mind engaged.

5) Write in public whenever quieter venues aren't available or even if they are. This at first may seem difficult, but you will learn to "zone out" and ignore distractions. Then you will be able to write anywhere, at any time.

**The Extreme Novelist Contract:** As an Extreme Novelist, I agree to the Rules as outlined above. These include daily writing sessions, with the exception of one day off each week. I'll also keep an open mind to suggestions in this book and from other sources. These are *creative options* that I may choose to accept or not. Suggestions are not personal criticism of me, my ideas, or my writing.

_____     _____
      Signature          Date

Please print, complete, and sign your contract and then post it where you'll see it often during the next eight weeks.

Because many writers live a great distance from the Washington, DC, area, and therefore are unable to sit in my classroom, I'm writing this book for them. (For you?) Some elements of this distance version of The Extreme Novelist program will need to differ a little from the original. I can't sit down with you and chat about the scene you just wrote. And face-to-face support from class members isn't possible. But the essence of the program remains, which is *the development of self-discipline and confidence through tips offered in this book.* This initial discipline will provide a model for your days, giving you the support you need to make writing a priority in your life.

Now is the time to sign yourself up for eight weeks of aggressive and dedicated writing. If you do, and you honestly stick with the program, I know you'll be thrilled with how quickly, and relatively painlessly, you'll accumulate pages for your novel.

### *Honor Your Accountability*

When I first started thinking about and devising The Extreme Novelist course, I told a friend that I expected no one would sign up for it. "This in-your-face, hard-line approach, the contract and all—it's going to scare everyone away!"

Although I believed that this sort of help was exactly what many would-be novelists *needed* to succeed at writing their books, I really did worry that prospective students would be repelled by the tone and no-nonsense ground rules. No one wants to be ordered around. Nobody wants to be *told* what to do.

But he encouraged me to at least try. So I turned in my proposal for the course, which was approved by the director. The Extreme Novelist would be posted on the school's website and in the printed catalogue for the spring semester. I waited to see what would happen.

To my shock, the class filled almost as soon as the new semester's offerings were published. We had decided that fifteen students should be the maximum class size, that is, if anyone showed up for the party. And, apparently, they had! The center's program director suggested we start a wait list. When that grew to ten hopeful students, we added a second class for the current semester.

The course has now run three semesters each year, for six years. It's nearly always full and often is wait listed. I believe the reason The Extreme Novelist has become so popular is because a vast number of people, whose goal it is to write book-length fiction, recognize the importance of being responsible for their own success, at least to the extent that fate allows. We are accountable to others in our day jobs, and in our communities and families. Why not for our art?

If we decide we're going to write a book, possibly telling others of our plans, we need to back up our words with action. Unless we're actually *doing* something to support our vision, we can't fully believe in ourselves.

When Extreme Novelist students are in the classroom they are expected to share with the group information about how their writing week went. If they didn't stick with the program and managed fewer than their minimum  ninety-minutes-a-day, they usually are honest enough to admit it. If they worked for  ninety minutes or more each day but failed to produce what they consider a reasonable number of pages, they are encouraged to speculate as to why this might be.

Classmates may sympathize with valid excuses ("My mother was hospitalized, and I needed to be with her.") They also learn to recognize a fellow writer who intentionally, or unintentionally, distracts himself with activities other than writing. Furthermore, class members who are less than successful at meeting their writing obligations often receive suggestions and extra support from others in the class. Everyone's life is different, and yet we all face time-management challenges.

The bottom line is this. By following this program, writers are encouraged to be frank with themselves about their priorities and dedication to their writing. If they aren't putting in the time, they know they can't expect to get the book written anytime soon. No one wants to be the writer who admits to having spent twenty years struggling to write one book.

### *Not a Conventional Workshop*

I'm sometimes asked by a prospective student if we will be critiquing each other's work in class. This "workshopping" technique is familiar to many who have taken other writing courses. (Students bring sections of their novel to be read by the group and then commented on.) When I tell them "no workshopping in this course" some are relieved, others disappointed.

The reason for not including time to read and analyze each other's manuscripts should be obvious. Each author needs to focus on his or her own book. The emphasis is on growing their story and making pages. If we fill our heads with the plots and characters of others in the class (or spend time doing critical analyses of published authors), we won't get our own writing done. This is precious time we need to defend in order to reach our goal of a rough draft in eight weeks.

On the other hand, hearing a little about each other's books keeps the class interesting and friendly, encouraging students to make connections with one or more writers with whom they feel particularly comfortable. Ultimately, the bonds created in the classroom can help members build a close support system that will extend past the end of the formal class meetings.

This bonding experience between writers has often worked better than I'd hoped. I regularly hear from former students who, years after having taken the course, let me know that they are still in touch with and support the writing progress of two, three, or more of their former classmates.

But you don't need to be in a physical classroom to receive or give this sort of support—writer to writer. Finding other writers in your area and connecting with them on a casual or more formal basis, that works too.

### *Expect of Yourself Only So Much*

To be honest, I assumed from the start that not every writer would complete their draft within two months. We were setting an aggressive pace. I was expecting a lot of my writers. But if each of my students mastered the process for: 1) Fully engaging in their creative project, and 2) Making their writing a priority—they would then be able to work independently for the additional few weeks needed to complete their draft.

Only after a full draft is done should the finer touches of fiction be addressed. We have to accept the idea that no one can expect to dash off a story that will be publishable, let alone readable, without revision. Revision is the detail work; it needs to come later. First we tackle the broad view of our story, to provide structure. Once we have that framework securely in place, the revision that makes the writing beautiful, and the book memorable, becomes possible.

*The key to success in completing the writing of a novel is expecting only so much ourselves as writers at one time.* When creating a rough draft, we're not looking for perfection. It's enough to just get a grip on the story.

### *Why Not One Perfect Page a Day?*

I realize there are those who encourage fiction writers to pen just one polished and perfect page a day. That's about 250 words when typed in a standard format (e.g., Times New Roman, 12pt. font, double-spaced lines). On the surface, it seems quite doable.

Proponents of this technique point out, quite accurately, that at the end of a year the author should have a book of roughly 365 pages. Best of all, this approach seems undemanding and very straightforward. Who can't write a measly 250 words a day? And, most thrilling of all, no revisions!

How very tempting.

Frankly, this slow-mo process of getting a book on paper would drive me crazy. I might *try* to write perfect prose, but that's not what would happen. I would weigh every word I wrote, second guess every plot decision, constantly criticize my progress. The Voices would seize control, their taunts attacking me at every turn of phrase: "Don't even think of calling this good writing. It's crap. It's laughable! No one will want to read this." By the end of a few weeks, I'd be so frustrated by falling short of that unattainable label "Perfection" that I'd give up.

If we think about the way our brains work, it becomes easy to see why this one perfect, carefully crafted page-a-day approach is doomed to failure. Studies support the fact that the human brain does not have an on/off switch. Neither does it possess the ability to shift at will from creative to critical thinking.

Once we allow our brain free rein to creatively spin a tale, it kicks into high gear. If we don't interrupt its work, our little gray cells (if you're a Poirot fan, you'll know about those) will keep us involved in building our story. We'll become more and more involved as new ideas for scenes or characters spontaneously generate in our subconscious then show up on our pages as we type.

It's almost as if the story is writing itself! We call this *living in the book*. It's an amazing feeling. We become so fiercely connected with our story that we can't wait for the next chance to write more.

However, let's pretend there actually *is* a switch in our brain. We can then place an order: "Stop creating. For the next thirty minutes I want you to work on making this scene better." In short, we're asking our brain to accept a different job, that of literary critic and editor. What happens then?

Within minutes, we discover that we've become ensnared in a web of searching out grammatical errors and weak wording. We're compelled to polish and make the text flawless. Which isn't altogether bad. It's just the wrong *time* for tackling this task. The story hasn't been fully crafted; fussing over details at this point is premature. We haven't yet addressed the big-picture elements of our tale.

Realizing this, we may frantically try to shift back into creative mode, but it's hard to do that now because we've lost that lovely creative energy surge. We're trapped in revision mode and find it impossible to extricate ourselves.

This is the typical pattern we referred to earlier, of the novelist who can't finish a book. He gives up and lays the project aside. Maybe he gives up on writing entirely.

Alternatively, the author may react to The Voices by placing blame for imperfections on the story rather than on his writing. He puts this particular story idea aside to work on what he hopes may be a better one. This cycle of starting and stopping work on one book or another can continue for years. (Sound familiar?) The result is a closetful of incomplete manuscripts. Every semester students sit in my classroom who are cyclic writers. They've begun and given up on two, five, ten novels.

Other students confess, "I've been working on one book for over twenty years, in my head or on paper. I just want to get it finished and move on." Working on a single book for this long shows true dedication. The writer is to be commended. However, this long of a journey is unnecessary and inefficient. In many cases it's also terribly traumatic and frustrating to the author, who can't understand why he isn't able to complete his novel.

In each case, the true blame usually lies in The Perfection Myth. The author is trying to make those first few pages, scenes, or chapters perfect before moving on through the book. This is just plain wrong. Most novelists who can't complete a book fail to do so because they keep rewriting the same first chapter or two. They are trying to make the prose "good enough," all the while sensing they're not up to the task.

The truth is, by the end of a chapter or two, no author can possibly know everything she needs to know about an entire story, about each and every character she will introduce or the implications of each dramatic scene. We are still learning the story. We need to get a handle on the scope and shape of the entire book. That's what a first draft is for. Before you criticize and correct the flaws in your writing, you have to get the dang thing down on paper or typed into a digital file. Only then will you have something to lovingly massage into a work of art.

This I promise: *Out of chaos will come beautiful order and an amazing book. But first, you have to write rough.*

### Take One Bite at a Time

To avoid burning out in the early chapters or middle of a novel—as well as to thwart the intimidation that accosts us when we contemplate the magnitude of our book-writing endeavor—we need to take little bites out of this literary feast.

One bite. Chew. One bite. Chew. Then digest.

The first bite is planning the story, as much as it can be planned. Call this a plot synopsis, an outline, a battle plan—whatever you like. It's a process that combines your natural creative impulses with practical decisions.

The second bite will follow in the form of the very rough draft we've been discussing.

26

Yes, there are some writers who are capable of giving their characters full rein and letting the story spill organically from a character-author brain union of sorts. But the end result of these unplanned stories is often unsatisfactory and rife with inconsistencies and wandering plot lines that require major surgery. Massive, migraine-producing rewrites follow. Dozens of irrelevant pages, characters, or themes must be pruned from the manuscript. We can avoid that heartbreaking process by planning ahead, if only with broad brush strokes.

Another benefit of allowing ourselves a few prewriting decisions, and then a speedy initial draft without engaging our inner critic, is pure enjoyment of the writing process. Because we are asking less of ourselves at this stage of the writing, we feel open to inspiration and freewheeling imagination. One student described the sensations in this way: "It's almost as if the story is all there in my head. And I'm just taking dictation, just letting the images in my brain seep out through my fingertips as I type."

*Wonderful!*

This shows amazing insight into the process of creating a rough draft. She has allowed herself to enjoy the ride now that she is free of the pressure of perfection. It's during this drafting stage of the novel, supported by at least a loose outline, that we actually learn the scope of our story, ultimately arriving at a beginning, middle, and end—with the scenes sketched in to the best of our ability.

In addition, we meet and learn about our characters by placing them in scenes and allowing them to interact with each other and deal with the drama in which they're involved. We make decisions along the way, choosing to take the plot in one direction or another. We give characters traits that suit the plot. And with each decision we make, we build a story in our own unique way. We also make the task at hand easier for ourselves. Easier because there are fewer and fewer decisions to be made the deeper we move into the story.

Another way of looking at this early-draft process is by comparing it with the steps a landscape artist takes to produce a finished oil painting. A traditional painter first works in broad strokes, laying down a "wash" of color then overlaying it with the predominant images—mountains, a building, large tree, ocean, or field. These first shapes may appear fairly vague, just sketched in.

Shadows and intense patches of light appear. As the process continues, the artist adds layers of pigment, and the brush strokes become finer and finer, revealing ever more detail on the canvas. The final and most delicate touches are added with a fine-tipped brush.

This layering effect creates the finished painting. We can also layer our prose in order not to overwhelm our brain by expecting too much of it all at once.

### *Eight Weeks to a New Habit*

The week before a new semester begins, I ask my authors to commit themselves to an aggressive writing program for eight weeks. (You've already seen a modified version of the guidelines and contract I send to them.) In the first class I explain why The Extreme Novelist course runs for two months instead of two weeks or half a year.

Phillippa Lally, a health-psychology researcher at University College London, published the results of a study on the time required to establish a new habit in the *European Journal of Social Psychology.* She had asked each participant to choose one new habit. These ranged from drinking a bottle of water with each meal to incorporating a daily run into their schedule. The goal was to determine when the urge to do the new habit became automatic. The answer: sixty-six days, which is just about the length of the Extreme Novelist course.

Keep in mind that what we're trying to do as Extreme Novelists is to establish a new and automatic habit of daily writing, because we know this is the best way to: 1) Consistently build pages and finish a novel, and 2) Stay "in the book," thereby making the writing process easier and more pleasant.

A reassuring additional result of the study, stated in an article in the *Huffington Post* in April 2014, was this: Lally learned that missing a day's activity "did not materially affect the habit formation process." Therefore, it doesn't matter if you screw up now and then! You haven't destroyed your chances of building that great new writing habit. You simply pick up your writing schedule where you left off.

The longer you keep working to ingrain the habit, the easier it becomes to make your writing time an automatic part of your day.

After a while, completing your daily quota of pages becomes as routine as brushing your teeth.

Also encouraging is the idea that we needn't pressure ourselves to get fully locked into a strict schedule within a few months. Eight-to-ten weeks is an average to establish habit. If we relax and enjoy the progress we are making in our daily writing, however small it may sometimes seem, the habit will come of its own accord.

In fact, if you believe you can only squeeze thirty minutes of uninterrupted writing into your days, then write for thirty minutes each day. Within a few weeks you'll find it nearly impossible to make yourself stop at half an hour. Your brain will urge you (plead with you!) to let it luxuriate longer in the story you love.

Let's think a little more about how habits work for or against us.

In general, the more complicated or ingrained a habit, the longer it will take for us to quit it. The most difficult of these habits include addictions to tobacco, alcohol, and drugs. For those we may need professional help. But our writing habits are much less resistant to change, not to mention less harmful. For the sake of turning yourself into a productive and happy Extreme Novelist, assume you will need around eight weeks to make the transformation.

If you are a person who happens to be particularly resistant to change, becoming fully engaged in the program may actually take three or even four months. Inevitably, though, if you are persistent in following a daily writing practice, the hard work of getting yourself seated at the desk gives way to a strong physical and emotional urge to hit the keyboard.

External pressures such as travel, work commitments, or family complications do sometimes make it impossible to write for a day or two. I joke with my students about wanting them to feel emotional distress, maybe even pain, when they are kept from their writing. This may sound cruel on my part, but experiencing discomfort on nonwriting days is actually a good sign.

Former students have contacted me to report their moodiness or eruptions of temper as a result of being kept from, or interrupted during, their writing times. It's a similar reaction to that of an athlete who suffers an injury and feels anxious and frustrated when unable to train for a period of weeks. We are compelled to respond to the habit of running or swimming or writing because it has become a part of who we are.

Thus, it's wise to be flexible in our expectations of what we'll accomplish during the first two months of following a program of rapid daily writing. Some writers feel well established in their new routine at the six-week mark or even earlier. Others report, after the end of our formal classes, that it took them an additional two or three weeks to feel fully engaged in the process.

### Why Ninety Minutes?

The goal of ninety minutes writing time, six days out of seven, is purely arbitrary. Every writer is unique. Graduates frequently modify their personal "rules" to best fit their lives. Many get so caught up in their stories they won't take even the one day off they're allowed. Some don't want to stop working at the ninety-minute minimum each day. They're just hitting their stride at the two- or three-hour mark.

One author felt her optimum time was four hours, with a break in the middle for bathroom and coffee. Another preferred to focus on actual pages completed rather than time spent at the keyboard. He had learned that he tended to waste time sitting at his computer and musing over dozens of options for each scene—screen staring. As a result, he set his daily minimum production at eight pages per day. By focusing on pages produced, rather than time seated at his desk, he kept up a steady flow of scenes and chapters, while still reassuring himself that they needn't be perfect. Not just yet.

Ninety minutes works well for many writers because it gives them ample time to warm up to the day's task and make some real progress before they need to step away from the keyboard to deal with the rest of their life. It's also enough time to break into manageable segments if they are unable to secure a single, daily block of writing time.

You can create the ideal program for *your* daily writing. We'll discuss many more good options in a later chapter. For now, let's set a tentative goal of committing to write six days a week, at least ninety minutes each day, for eight weeks, as stated in your contract, just as your fellow Extreme Novelists do in the Washington, DC, class.

If you stick with the program, at the end of eight weeks you will have developed strong writing muscle, in addition to a habit that makes you every bit as professional as any published novelist.

***Your Turn***

Now that you know the basic drill—write ninety minutes or more each day, six days a week, without criticizing yourself—why not make today the first day of your eight-week experience as an Extreme Novelist? If you start now, as you continue reading this book for additional tips and support, you'll already be making progress toward completing your novel.

Whether you begin in earnest today, tomorrow, or next week, mark the day on your calendar then count off eight weeks so that you can celebrate how far you've come when that day arrives.

(A word of caution: Have you said to yourself, "I'll start my eight weeks in the summer, when I have more time." Or, "Maybe after the holidays I can begin." Or, "I think this will work after I retire." If so, you're already using delaying tactics that will likely interfere with following the program. There is no perfect day to begin. Even after you begin there will be challenges to getting in your ninety minutes. Best to dive right in!)

## Chapter 3: Becoming an Extreme Novelist

### *Find Your High-Energy Time of Day*

You may point out, quite reasonably, that you work long hours at your day job. You have a family. You have many important commitments. And you are exhausted! "I can't possibly add another hour or more to my already crammed days."

I understand. At times, that's how we all feel.

The first step toward making writing time is to stop the vicious cycle of commitment and guilt we all experience. Because we really *do* want to write our books. And not having time in our lives to do what we long for—well, that's simply unacceptable.

The solution is easier to explain than to accomplish, I admit, but it's definitely doable. If every hour of your day is already spoken for, then an activity (or time-waster) must be eliminated or downgraded to a lower priority. Only then will we make room in our lives for writing on a daily basis. A no-brainer, right?

The first step toward restructuring your days is to pinpoint the time of day when you naturally get the most work done with the least effort. Call this your *Power Hour*. It's also when your head is clearest, your subconscious is most willing to do at least some of the work for you, and creativity is at its height. But what is this magic hour when all of these abilities come together and are most available to us?

As individuals, we each have a unique high-energy time of day. The important thing to remember is: *Everyone* has an hour or more that is mentally supercharged and available for use. It's that ideal time of day when you know that, if you have one or two critical tasks to accomplish in the next twenty-four hours, that's when you need to do them.

Some people spend the first hour or two of their day checking off a few household chores, like picking up clutter or vacuuming. They know that if they don't do it then they won't get to it at all—or the job will feel all the more like drudgery when they're tired. Others of us have made a habit of browsing our Twitter feed, Facebook page, or favorite sites over morning coffee. This is our quiet time, the hour or two before our lives become hectic and less easy to control.

The truth is, on any given day, whatever plans we've made for writing are in danger of being interrupted by the demands of everything else going on in our lives. But if we discover and protect our power hour, using it solely for our writing, we can deal with the rest of life during the remaining twenty-two or so hours of the day.

Sometimes we just need to stop the treadmill, take a deep breath, and reclaim a small slice of our lives for our own use. This isn't a selfish act. It's an act of self-love. A joyful seizing of precious time to use for doing something we love. Don't let anyone tell you any different!

### *What is Your Power Hour?*

Are you an early bird, a night owl, or someone who's most alert and energized during the middle of the day?

As Extreme Novelists, we target times of day that are our most productive. Your Power Hour may be first thing in the morning or late at night. You may become ultraalert only after you've had a few hours to fully wake up, but before you become distracted by the day's inevitable "emergencies." Whenever it is, you will defend these ninety minutes (or more, if you like) with the ferocity of a mother lion protecting her cubs. This will be your prime time for writing, if at all possible.

Are there other times of the day or night that you notice you feel at least moderately energetic? Take note of all possibilities, even if you think that time is already dedicated to some other task.

I have come to realize that my prime writing time is always first thing in the day. I'm the ultimate morning person. The later in the day it gets, the less I get done. My mind becomes scattered, I'm easily distracted, and my stamina fades. I know that I must schedule the heavy-lifting mental tasks before noon. Any chore that's mindless and mechanical—you know, the stuff you can do in your sleep like wiping down kitchen countertops, defleaing the dog, mowing the lawn—is saved for after 3:00 p.m., because that's my "dead zone."

For years I have tried to explain to my family how much better and faster I can write first thing in the morning. I tell the man I'm married to now (very supportive, by the way), "Sweetie, if you will simply bring me a mug of hot tea, leave it on the bedside table, and then set my laptop on top of me in bed, I will put fingers to keyboard and write like the wind."

It's true! I write at least three times faster, without sacrificing quality, on waking. He humors me, sometimes, but often just smiles indulgently, not really believing me.

I admit, it does sound a little silly. But time and again, this system has worked for me. My second-best system involves staggering down to the kitchen, grabbing my hot beverage and the laptop, then retreating to bed or a comfy chair to write while I'm still in that woozy, semiwakeful state of early morning. I can write for an hour or two, concluding my writing time with many more pages logged in that day than if I'd allowed myself to do a handful of chores before writing. (It's always a huge mistake to check my e-mail first thing.)

I highly recommend wake-up writing!

Why does this work so well for many writers—even those who don't consider themselves morning people?

As we fully rouse ourselves to the business of the day we start remembering the things we hoped to accomplish that day. The dreaded mental list. If somebody else lives with us—we may be discussing their (and our) plans for the day. Perhaps another chore or three are added to the to-do list. ("If you could stop by the dry cleaner to pick up my suit while you're out? Oh, and we're out of milk and cat litter.") The longer we are awake, the more urgently life interferes with the stories in our head.

But wait! There is still another benefit, perhaps the best of all, to writing first thing in the morning.

*In this half-wakeful state our minds are free to journey, to take leaps of faith and try out fresh ideas.* By letting our subconscious take over some of the creative labor, by never turning on our self-critic (remember The Voices?), we can write faster, more freely, with far less interference from negative thoughts. This is a wonderful gift!

However, this first-thing-in-the-morning writing isn't the only way to fit working on your book into your day, particularly when time is really at a premium. Here are some methods my students and mentoring clients have adopted to help them get their novels written.

# THE EXTREME NOVELIST

**The Commuter**—Frank lives in Maryland. He has a typical commute from the suburbs and takes the Metro into Washington, DC, daily. He writes for forty minutes on his way into the city on the subway in the morning, and another forty minutes on his return trip. He uses a tablet propped on his knees, most of the time, but will sometimes switch to his phone for taking down notes, searching the Internet for information, or sketching a new scene. He also likes to write another thirty minutes or so before bed, which preps him for the next day's writing. In this way, without ever sitting down at a desk to write, he gets in nearly two hours of writing each day. And most of it is scrounged up from otherwise fallow time.

**The Mom**—Marilyn is a working professional woman with two young children. To say her work days are hectic would be an understatement. A demanding full-time job constantly competes with time she needs (and wants) to spend at home with her children. She picks her writing times carefully. She usually manages to write for at least thirty minutes during her lunch hour. If she can't close her office door and ensure she isn't interrupted, she leaves her own department and sits in an empty office to write. She also works on her book for an hour immediately after her children have been tucked into bed. By the last hour or two of the day she admits to being "pretty worn out" and unable to concentrate on her story, so she uses this time to do a load of laundry and tidy up the house to prepare for the next day. She says, "I can still keep my head in my story while I'm doing mindless chores. And at least I know by then I've gotten in my requisite ninety minutes a day."

**Young & Restless**—Gregory is an enthusiastic twenty-something author. He has three roommates who are boisterous and demanding of his time socially. He complains that he can't possibly write in the apartment; the interruptions are constant. But he has found alternate "offices" for his writing times. There's a coffee shop within walking distance, just down the street. That's where he writes most of the time. The Quiet Room at the library is his second choice, although he prefers the coffee shop since he can have the beverage of his choice while he works. Besides, he likes knowing that famous authors throughout history have often favored neighborhood cafés, parks, bars, and restaurants while writing their novels. Following the tradition makes him feel he's a serious writer with a future in publication.

**My Personal Fave**—Here's one of my own Extreme Novelist tricks from the past. When my children were young, I had a full-time job in the headquarters of a large bank. I arrived early to get in thirty minutes of writing before my boss, and almost everyone else in the office, showed up. With half an hour under my belt and my brain charged with my story's plot, I was able to continue thinking about my characters, dreaming up sources of conflict, and constructing scenes in my head during the morning as I completed mundane tasks at my desk.

Come lunch time, when everyone else went to the cafeteria, I strolled outside to the parking lot and sat in my car. I'd brought my lunch so I could sit there and write for another thirty minutes or more. Now I had only another half hour to squeeze in to complete my ninety-minute writing goal for the day.

I might have been tired by the time I finished critical household chores and tucked the kids into bed that night—but I'd bring a cup of herbal tea or glass of wine to my favorite easy chair, flip open my laptop, and dive back into my story for a little while. In that relaxed position I was able to knock off another few pages, thus completing my ninety-minute commitment.

**The Loving Caretaker**—Jennifer lives with and cares for her elderly mother. She works in a real estate office in the town where they make their home. Before she leaves for work in the morning she sees to her mother's meals and personal needs for the day.

When Jennifer comes home in the early evening, her mother is eager for her company. They enjoy making and eating dinner together. But Jennifer's too tired to write immediately after her workday and a full meal, and she doesn't have the heart to isolate herself when her mother is so desperate for her company. So they visit for a while, and then Jennifer goes to bed at the same time as her mother: 9:00 p.m.—*after setting the alarm on her cell phone for 2:00 a.m.*

# THE EXTREME NOVELIST

When the phone gently jingles her awake, she gets up, makes herself a hot beverage, and sits down at the kitchen table to write. She works for at least an hour, or for as long as two, before returning to bed to sleep until 7:00 a.m., at which time she showers and dresses for work.

She tells me, "While researching my historical novel, I discovered that, before the twentieth century, people sometimes wrote about a First Sleep and Second Sleep. It was expected that one awoke during the night, read for a while or performed some task, then returned to bed for the rest of the night. This was considered normal." Jennifer likes returning to this older way of doing things, which suits her time-management challenges and helps her connect with the era she's writing about.

**Writing Sprints**—Many of my students target brief pockets of otherwise wasted time during their days—ten, fifteen minutes, or more. When used as a writing sprint these minutes generate more pages when totaled up at the end of a day. Waiting in the school car line, you can dash off a bit of dialogue or a scene. Sitting in a medical office waiting room, steal those fifteen minutes or more to work on character development. Waiting for a bus or subway, for a store to open, for the end of a child's sports practice, tutoring session, or music lesson—all of these lost minutes become opportunities to sprint for a page or more in your novel.

### *Learn to Live in the Book*

Jennifer, Frank, Marilyn, and Gregory have been living in their books. They might not always be able to protect their ideal high-energy time of day. Certain elements of their lives can't be altered. Their work hours aren't flexible. They have to be at their jobs, on time and ready to work. For them, as for many of us, there's no secluded cabin in the woods or other perfect writer's retreat. They need to make do with the time they manufacture in between the rest of life's demands.

If you can't dedicate at least  ninety minutes of your day in a single glorious chunk, use windows of time throughout your day as these writers have done. Shake up your schedule if you need to. Doing so is well worth a little planning and effort. But be spontaneous too by taking advantage of dead time when it happens. You'll be factoring into your life consistent creative time—minutes that add up and are *all your own!* The result is immensely rewarding; you are accomplishing what you've always dreamed of doing. You are a working writer.

In addition, if you are able to do your writing in the first moments of your day, you'll receive an extra jolt of satisfaction. No matter what else happens during your busy, demanding day—*your writing is done!* And once you've established your individual routine of writing at least six days a week, ninety minutes or more each day, you will be amazed at how quickly the rough draft of your story grows.

### *What If Disaster Strikes?*

Life sometimes goes horribly wrong. Major life-altering events can wreak havoc with our writing schedule. The trick is to recognize the difference between a true emergency and the daily time-nibbling grind that snatches away minutes, then hours, of our writing time.

We're talking about the death of a loved one, serious illness or hospitalization of the author or—less tragically but no less disruptive—emotional time-sucks like selling a home or changing jobs. These are events that can't be ignored and are often spirit crushing. Because our heart is deeply troubled, or demands are being made on us that we can't put off, we find it difficult to focus on anything but the most pressing tasks. Writing anything, much less a novel, feels almost impossible.

I can sympathize if this is your current situation. However, it may be helpful if I share one thought with you: *Some of the most challenging times in my life have been made more bearable by having a story to retreat into.* Your novel can become a gift during stressful, difficult, or sad times. Your book provides a private place into which you can escape, to be distracted or even soothed.

Here's just one example:

Back in the year 2000, my family physician advised me not to put off back surgery any longer. I'd been diagnosed with scoliosis as a teenager. Over the decades since then, the curvature of my spine had deteriorated, worsening drastically. She sent me to an orthopedic surgeon, who told me that my condition was "life-limiting." In other words I'd likely have fewer years in this life that I love if I did nothing. Furthermore, I'd probably spend the last of them in a wheelchair. And the longer I waited, the more difficult, and risky, the surgery would be.

It seemed I had no choice but to "go under the knife." I agreed to move ahead with plans for my hospital stay. No matter how scary it sounded, I needed to do this—for my long-term health and to spend more productive years with the people I loved. My surgeon explained that I should expect a full year for recovery. I wouldn't be able to drive for months. I also would need strong painkillers until I could cope with the drastic changes in my body structure and the "hardware" inside of me. To say this was terrifying is to put it mildly.

How would the pain, heavy medication, and recovery time interfere with my ability to think, to create? I had signed contracts with firm deadlines for *three* books, all within post-surgery recovery time. If I wanted to be paid, I needed to somehow tough it out and get the books written. Curtailing my income wasn't an option.

I had the surgery and came home to live on the ground floor of my little townhouse. With the help of a friend, my bed had been moved downstairs into the living room before I went into the hospital. I wasn't supposed to do stairs for at least a month. I quickly discovered that I could sit up at my desk and type for no more than a few minutes at a time before I had to lie down again. That left me two options. I could type standing up or I could type lying down.

Standing up was manageable for about twenty minutes at a time. I wasn't sure if it was even possible to lie flat on my back and type. Searching online I found a gadget called a *Laid-back Laptop* desk. This was a strange-looking wooden contraption with a tray to support a laptop computer and two zigzag, hinged legs that could be adjusted. The manufacturer claimed the user could lie in bed and type comfortably. I ordered the dang thing, hoping for the best.

It worked!

I could now stretch out flat on my back, tilting the laptop screen so that it was in front of my face. I could work comfortably for an hour or more before I needed to get up and do the exercises the physical therapist demanded of me. But the best thing I discovered was that, by keeping myself entertained and focused on my writing, I was able to reduce then ditch the painkillers much sooner than expected. And recovery time seemed to speed by as I lost myself in my stories. (By the way, I still use my reclining laptop desk as a restful alternative to sitting and typing.)

Years later when tragedy struck in the form of my mother's struggle with Alzheimer's, and her ultimate death, I soothed myself again by disappearing into my work-in-progress. I honestly can't think of a better use for storytelling than as a healing tool. Novels can be a place of respite for the mind and the soul, for both writer and reader.

I write fiction because, in this harsh and challenging world of bitter politics, heartless diseases, and sometimes cruel human beings, I need to take a break from reality. I suspect, based on the phenomenal annual sale of novels, that many people find that same sort of peace in the books they read.

If part of your motivation for writing is to give your readers experiences beyond their own realities, then know that you are doing them a great service. You are entertaining, teaching, broadening their horizons through your stories. But you are also giving them a place to go to when the going gets tough.

## Chapter 4: The Fear Factor

We've talked about the intimidation involved in writing fiction. Ugly voices warn us we are bound for failure. Naysayers delight in pointing out how hard it is to write good fiction. Should we actually complete such a staggeringly difficult project, publication will still be a long shot—or so they say. These malevolent messages gang up on us and stand in the way of our enjoying our art.

We can fight such intimidation in several ways. One is to simply not announce to the world, "I am writing *a book*!" Here's why that sometimes makes sense.

Students often tell me they began writing their novel with a spurt of inspiration and energy, thrilled with the prospect of becoming a published author. They became so excited they couldn't keep their new love to themselves, and so told friends and family. Once everyone knew about their secret dream, well-meaning people started voicing their support.

"When will the book be done?"

Or, "Didn't you start working on your novel almost a year ago? How soon can I read it?"

Now it's no longer a beloved dream, a secret passion. It's become an obligation. As with any obligation there comes pressure: *I said I was going to do this. I've invested all of this time in writing, and everyone knows it. What if I fail? I'll feel like such a fool.*

Let's think about this a little differently. Because this is an immense undertaking, the prospect of writing a novel is much more easily managed if we expect only so much of ourselves at a time. We said earlier, we need to take small bites. So, each day when we sit down to work, instead of thinking of "writing a book," we might say to ourselves something like: "All I am going to do today is write one scene. Just one little scene. A scene has a beginning, middle, and end. It's short. It has one or more characters in it. *I can do this!*"

This may sound rather simpleminded, but it's terribly important that you write freely, without feeling stressed and anxious. Hold onto the enjoyment of your craft. Today, write just three, seven, or ten pages (whatever you're capable of) without criticizing yourself. Don't look back and mess with what you wrote yesterday or last week. Don't worry about the chapters to come. None of that is your job at the moment.

*This is all I expect of myself today: a few pages.*

By releasing ourselves from the responsibility for everything except this one isolated scene, we can move by increments closer and closer to completion. After a week, you'll have a short stack of scenes. After a month, a much higher stack will sit on the desk.

A big enough pile of scenes makes a book. It's really that simple. As the pile grows, the fear diminishes, and eventually is banished.

Even better, the more we write, the better we get. We stack up hours, and those hours contribute to our earning the rank of "expert." No one is a born writer. It's all about practice. Here's how we know this...

### *Ten Thousand Hours to Become an Expert*

Malcolm Gladwell, author of the book *Outliers*, studied the lives of extremely successful people. He wanted to find out if there was such a thing as a naturally gifted person, someone destined to be successful, perhaps even great. Was fame in a particular field predestined for some, while other less talented souls needed to struggle harder to achieve even moderate success?

Gladwell tells of a team of psychologists in Germany who studied the lives of violinists. They looked at each musician's practice habits from childhood into their adult years. All of the violinists began taking lessons at five years of age, spending similar times at practice. But by age eight, some were working at their music less time and others more.

This divergence appears to be critical to success. What might be called the "elite" performers later in life had accumulated more than ten thousand hours of practice. Those who had risen not as high in their musical careers often had practiced only four thousand hours.

Even more fascinating, there seemed to be no musicians who were "naturals." That is, no one among those who had practiced far fewer than ten thousand hours rocketed to the top purely on their talent. Based on his studies, Gladwell states that it takes around ten thousand hours of doing something to achieve mastery in that chosen field.

So-called overnight wonders, like hitherto unknown authors who suddenly hit the *New York Times* bestseller lists (e.g., J.K. Rowling), have put in thousands of hours honing their craft. They are the high achievers of the writing world, mirroring the success of people in other fields, like Bill Gates, Paul McCartney, Itzhak Perlman, and a galaxy of sports stars. They didn't just work harder than others to become good at what they do, *they fell in love with their work*. They did it continually, some may say obsessively, because it became a part of who they are. They felt driven to do it.

We can learn from Gladwell. What he's saying means that virtually anyone can become exceedingly good at what they strive to do.

You want to become a novelist whose stories are published and enjoyed by thousands of readers? Then write *a lot*, as much as you can, and daily. The more you practice, the better writer you'll become. Throwing yourself, body and soul, into the creation of your stories, studying the techniques of other authors, spending time immersed in your plot and the world you've created on paper, and turning out pages—this is all part of accumulating your ten thousand hours.

As a bonus, when we write fast, screening out the negative voices, letting our subconscious do much of the work during the initial first and rough draft, we make it easier for us to fall in love with our art. It stays *fun*! We are no longer intimidated by the challenging task at hand because we understand more about the process. All of this makes us want to write more.

The truth is, you don't have to have achieved your ten thousand hours to get published. It doesn't magically happen at that very moment. When I had many fewer hours under my writer's belt, I felt a bit of a fraud when I received my first book contract (even though I'd already been writing for years).

I knew I wasn't writing as spectacularly as many authors whose work I loved. Maybe I never would. But while I was practicing my art, some of my books found publishers. The more I wrote, the better I got. The better I got, the more books sold and the fewer were rejected. And somewhere along the line, I began to feel I had become "legitimate."

When you're an Extreme Novelist, writing at least ninety minutes a day, six days a week, you are working rapidly toward your ten thousand hours. If you continue putting in that minimum time, after a year you will have accumulated 468 hours. I know, that's just a dent in reaching expert status. But if you treat working on your fiction like a job (as professional authors do) and you were to write forty hours each week for a year, you would have added more than two thousand hours to your total. In just five years, according to Gladwell's theory, you would have achieved mastery of your craft. Can't log in that many hours? You might try for twenty hours a week.

It's a rather straightforward process, really. Write a lot. Pay attention to the lessons from those who have gone before you. And don't listen to The Voices.

### *Don't Look Back!*

In accordance with the Extreme Novelist rules, we don't look back at what we've already written. Writing quickly and making consistent forward progress gives our subconscious free rein to work for us. We're not aiming for perfection in this first round. We're merely getting the essence of the story down on paper. We're learning about the characters—who they are, what makes them tick, where they came from, and what they want or need that's driving them to act as they do.

If we give ourselves permission to write forward, without paying a great deal of attention to fact-checking, grammar, or spelling— that's okay. We know we'll have plenty of time to return to these pages and caress them into beautiful prose. With this reassurance we free ourselves of the pressure that we ourselves, and the world, try to put upon us when we take on the demanding task of writing a book.

"But," you may say, "what if I realize five chapters into the novel that I've wandered from my original plot? What if the story spins off in another direction or goes horribly wrong, or suddenly I have an even better idea for a character or a scene than what I've already written? Don't I need to go back and fix previous scenes so the new idea will fit and make sense?"

No!

"Or maybe add new characters?"

No!

"Don't I need to revise at least *some* at this point?"

*No!*

Beware. This is a trap. Unless you started out writing a sentimental love story but you're now whipping through blood-soaked scenes whereby vicious serial-killer aliens decapitate innocent earthlings—no, you shouldn't stop to rewrite or patch up already-written scenes. If you do, chances are you'll get sucked into the revision trap before your full draft is done. And there you'll stay, fussing over those first few chapters and failing to move forward to completion of the story.

What you *can* do, however, is this.

Very quickly (as if a taxi is waiting outside your door with the meter running) locate the place in your manuscript, either on-screen or in a printed version, where you think you might need to add a scene, character, event, or different plot element. Jot down and highlight a quick note to yourself. Something along the lines of:

*Remember: I need to add Mickey Black to this action, to establish he was here at the time of the murder.*

Or: *Create a scene here that shows Annabelle and Melanie running into each other in the grocery store.*

Then pick up the writing at your farthest point and carry on with your draft.

Now that you've planted the idea in your brain (by leaving reminders for revision time), you can move the story along as if those changes were already in place. Later on, if you envision still more changes to earlier pages, stop only long enough to drop in similar suggestions to yourself. Then continue writing forward.

*Changes belong in the revision process.* That's when you'll coordinate scenes, move them into the most effective order. You'll fine-tune your characters' personalities, check to be sure they're in the scenes they need to be in, and not in those where they get in the way of the drama. You'll be free to primp and polish your prose to your heart's content and make the story work logically for the reader.

Think about it. Does it make sense to stop and add material to already-drafted sections of the book before you reach the end of the story? Isn't it reasonable to assume that this sparkly new idea that just struck you today may also be discarded when you hit on an even newer, more intriguing idea? Best to just leave the note. That way, you won't be tempted to lose yourself in chapter 2, yet again, when you've already made it all the way to chapter 10 but have another twenty chapters to go.

Remember the Bible story about Lot and his family fleeing the sinful city of Sodom? They were instructed by angels not to look back. Was it because temptation would be their undoing and they might change their minds and stay in the sinful city? Lot obeyed, but his wife did not. As punishment for looking back, she was turned into a pillar of salt.

Don't become a pillar of salt, stuck in early chapters and unable to finish your book.

Once aware of the risk of looking back, some of my students are unwilling to risk even a quick peek to dash off a note to themselves. Instead, they keep a separate journal with thoughts and instructions to themselves about possible corrections and additions to specific pages. Or they create a new file on their computer where they record ideas about alterations in drafted scenes and possibilities for scenes to come.

These spontaneous suggestions, quickly noted so as not to interrupt the flow of writing, will become particularly valuable later in the process of refining the story. You'll already have a good deal of your revision work laid out in the form of assignments.

### *It's All About the Questions*

Writing fiction is all about asking, and then answering, questions. Hundreds and hundreds of questions.

What does my main character want out of life?

How should my character react to this threat?

What setting will be most effective for the plot I have in mind?

What color gown would my heroine be most likely to choose?

Should I kill off this character or let her live?

Questions fly at you in an endless stream as you write. Don't let them throw you. No single answer is "right." Many answers are capable of making fantastic stories. The process of asking and answering questions is how we create fiction. It's also how we hold our readers' interest and earn their appreciation.

Listen to the questions that come to you. Answer them as best you can. But don't fret over one if at first it stumps you. Sometimes it takes considerable thought to arrive at an answer that suits the story. The possibilities are endless, and no single answer is the "right" one. That's part of the fun of fiction and one of the ways authors are able to keep readers guessing.

Remember: *For the moment, your job is simply to type.* In this way, moving quickly through both good and bad writing days, telling the story as best you can, you'll reach the end of your draft. Then you'll have before you a structure and a roughed out manuscript for your whole book. A plot that moves and is uniquely yours. Characters that you have come to know and now can delve into more deeply and chisel into exquisite shape.

### *Just Type*

At a writing conference some years back, I sat in the audience between my own speaking appearances and listened to a panel of my favorite mystery authors. I'm not sure who came out with the statement that brought down the house, but it went something like this:

"Writing is a lot like making love—you have to keep your hands moving."

Or was it fingers? I don't recall. But I like the image, and I think it makes sense in more ways than one.

You are, after all, falling in love with your own story as you write. But there's also that tactile connection between your fingers and the keyboard. Stroke a series of keys, and a word appears that wasn't there a moment ago. Magic!

There's something else about this body/mind link that's interesting. I'm not a scientist, so I can't tell you why what I'm about to say is true, but I've seen this happen so often that I believe it. As we move our hands and fingers through the motions of typing, ideas come more easily to the brain. Fresh concepts, vivid details, bits of dialogue rise up out of nowhere. It's when we cease typing, or moving the pen across the page, and sit staring at the screen while we strain to come up with an amazing idea that we feel blocked.

The fact is, even if you *think* things aren't going well with the book and your writing isn't anywhere close to brilliant—your brain continues to automatically churn out new solutions to your questions, *as long as you keep on writing*. Beloved characters, possibilities for exciting conflict, and unexpected plot twists come to mind without your putting much effort into the process. Therefore, doesn't it make sense to keep feeding your brain these sensory jolts to enable it to continue working for you?

And what about those days when you just don't feel like writing?

Be a pro. Professional writers work whether they are in the mood or not. It's their job. If you want it to be your job, feeling *inspired* is not a requirement. You will sit down and perform your daily writing tasks.

Neither does it matter whether or not you feel particularly excited about your story on a specific day. It makes no difference whether you got a great eight hours' sleep last night or the baby kept you up half the night. If you are an Extreme Novelist, you will still place butt in chair and fingers on keyboard, and make your pages for the day.

Your job is to tell your story, as much as you know of it, and as quickly as you can. It's as simple as that.

### *Your Turn*

Have you started writing in earnest? Are you building your story, one day at a time, ninety minutes or more each day? On the average, how many pages are you managing to write each day? Everyone is different when it comes to writing speed. Of course writers who spend three or more hours a day writing, as opposed to ninety minutes, will accumulate pages faster.

Writing fiction is such a personal endeavor that only you can arrive at a schedule that works for you. All that matters is that you are writing freely, not overthinking your plot and paper people, and putting in the time, consistently. Even if all you can write is two pages a day (five words), you'll have twenty-four thousand words of a draft at the end of eight weeks. That's enough for a rough version of a novella. If you want to make it a book, you can revise upward from that, doubling or tripling your word count by fleshing out details as you revise.

*NaNoWriMo* (National Novel Writing Month) participants often write 1,667 words a day, in order to draft a fifty-thousand-word novel in the thirty days of November. One of my writing friends drafts 1–3 pages on weekdays, but picks up his pace on weekends, when he usually can write 6–7 pages each day. I usually try to do ten pages a day, to give myself the best chance of completing my first draft within eight weeks. But that's because I mostly write rather long books.

Push yourself on some days to get in just one extra page above your average. But don't beat yourself up if you fail to always hit your mark. Writing fiction should be fun.

Keep up the good work!

## Chapter 5: Plotting

You may have read or heard somewhere that there are two types of fiction writers: *Plotters* and *Pantsers*. Each breed will defend their technique vehemently as the only possible way to write, at least for them.

Plotters enjoy thinking about their stories before they begin writing—coming up with characters' names and descriptions, devising sources of conflict, dreaming up interesting settings, and planning scenes. They feel more comfortable with the safety net of a written outline (plot synopsis), narrative summary, or perhaps visual organizational tools such as a timeline or family tree. In short, they like to have a road map they can follow as they write.

Pantsers—those who write "by the seat of their pants"— prefer to start out with a premise or theme, or maybe just one character or event as the source of their inspiration. Pantsers start writing with a minimum of preparation, then enjoy letting their story develop organically, without the constraints of a formal outline, adding in more characters or situations as they move from scene to scene. This is freewheeling creativity.

If you are the type of author who can do pantsing well—develop a novel out of thin air and pure inspiration, then let the characters decide matters for themselves—more power to you. I am in awe of you! Seriously. Because I *can't* do it.

In fact, I'd venture to say that only a very small percentage of all fiction writers are able to write really effectively without preparation. More often than not, if we don't plan ahead we run into plot or characterization or logic problems that slow us down, bring us to a complete halt, or drop us into a rabbit hole of confusion. If climbing out of the hole becomes too difficult, we find the writing more painful than rewarding. We might even become so frustrated that we give up. Our novel dies an early death.

To me, writing without a plan for my story is like performing a circus high-wire act. I'm a hundred feet above the ring, without a net. I'm scared out of my mind! I can't write that way. I long for the security that comes from having a simple, easy-to-follow outline I can refer to if I begin to worry about wandering from the core of my story or forget where I am in it.

A *narrative synopsis* is a form of outline. (Forget about the classic format with Roman numerals and uppercase/lowercase letters. This is much looser and more fun.) A novelist's outline is a road map the author creates for herself as a working model. Here's an example of what this sort of plotting sounds like:

*Elizabeth stands on the deck of the sailing ship. It's 1609, and she's traveling with her mistress to Jamestown, Virginia, when a terrible storm attacks the ship in the middle of the Atlantic. The passengers and crew struggle to keep the boat afloat. After three frantic days bailing and stuffing leaks with anything the passengers and crew can find, the storm abates and the ship runs aground on a coral reef off the coast of an uninhabited island in the dreaded Bermudas. All 149 onboard make it safely to shore, but now their ship is wrecked and useless.*

This paragraph describes the opening scenes of *The Gentleman Poet*, one of my novels based on real historical events. As you can see, the intent of the outline or synopsis is to reveal, in present tense, who is doing what and how the plot evolves. It's not intended to be a squished-up version of every scene in the entire book.

A synopsis mentions only the main plot points and central characters. It tracks turning points, climaxes small and large, gives us the essence of the story. The synopsis also is a valuable guide for the author, pointing the way from Incident A to Incident B, and all the way to the end of the story at Z.

As we write the actual story, following the trail, spurts of inspiration will occur to us. And because our outline is flexible, allowing for changes and additions along the way, we can take advantage of those marvelous twists of plot and vivid details that come to us later in the process. We're not locked into a rigid plan that stifles our creative impulses.

Furthermore, when writing a plot outline, there's no need to include dialogue. Whereas in the book itself we attempt to "show, don't tell," here we are *supposed* to tell. Not only does this sort of loose narrative planning take away a great deal of self-doubt about the direction of a story, it allows the author to write anywhere in the book. And that's a very helpful option.

For instance, if you happen *not* to be in the mood for writing the particularly emotional and complex scene that comes next in your story, you can skip over that scene for the moment. Save it for another day. Instead, you might choose to write a love scene, a humorous episode, or the entertaining climax of your story. You can jump from action that takes place near the beginning to a scene in the middle or one toward the end of the novel before returning to that sticky scene that was hanging you up.

When I'm feeling a little tired I like to pick myself up by writing a very active scene in my current story. Or I might take advantage of a blue-funk day and write my less-than-chipper mood into a scene where my main character is also feeling a little (or a lot ) low. Writing any place in the book we're inclined is truly liberating. As a plus, it relieves the tendency to tense up while tackling such a big, demanding job as a book.

Again, we're choosing small bites while telling ourselves we are allowed to play. We're having fun and writing what we want to write, while feeling safe. We're on track. We're making progress, creating pages, in control of the story.

If you're one of many writers who fear they might not be able to pull off this crazy novel-writing gig, then take a little more time musing about where you want your story to go, and what you want it to be. We're less intimidated by a challenging writing project when we've answered some of the questions that will inevitably come up while shaping a book.

This isn't *only* about emotional security. We're naturally concerned about the inevitable revisions. Although I generally love the process of revising for the opportunity to turn rough writing into something spectacular for my readers, I don't want to make the revisions any harder for myself than is necessary. If I totally shoot from the hip while penning my first draft, I know there will be many more missteps and a lot more gristle to be cut away from the meat of my prose.

When we plot before writing we are actually building into a first draft a truer version of what eventually will become the finished novel. There's less to change or correct, less to toss out or add in later. On the other hand, if we give ourselves unlimited freedom to choose from among dozens of paths during the first draft, we'll be loading extra work onto the back end of the writing process, necessitating many more subsequent drafts. Why would I want to do that to myself?

Overall, we'll surely spend less time and energy if we do at least a little planning before starting to write. Just get the basics of your story down on paper or saved into a digital file. Who are the main characters? What conflict drives this plot? Where does the tale begin and end? The more you know and write down, the firmer your book's working platform will be.

### *Length Matters*

I always warn my students to keep track of their word count. That's because I once had to cut sixty pages from a finished novel for a big-name publisher. It wasn't because I'd done anything wrong. For reasons neither I nor my agent understood, the publisher's legal department had made a mistake and put the wrong word count in the contract.

I was writing according to what I *thought* the publisher wanted—a much longer book. But the editor refused to accept the novel as it stood (and therefore pay me the portion of my advance due on acceptance) until I cut the extra pages. My agent said her hands were tied. I had no choice but to slash away. It was a horrid bloodletting.

This kind of cutting and reshaping of a novel is agonizing. Usually it can be avoided if you are aware of the preferred length of books within your genre and keep track of your running word count. You've toiled over those words, those precious pages. You don't want to suffer the pain of having to trash them.

Many new writers today end up doing just that. They write without paying attention to how long or short the book may end up.

Why is word count important?

It's a matter of production costs. The longer a book, the more it costs the publisher for paper, editing, and physical manufacture of the book. The price has to remain competitive or readers simply won't pay for your novel.

As it stands, the price to consumers of hardcover books has risen astronomically. Even trade paperbacks hover between $15 and $20 each. At those rates, it becomes difficult for most of us to afford more than an occasional book to feed our hunger for stories. (One reason for the rapid rise in e-book popularity?)

Many authors, having seen fat, lush adventures like the Harry Potter stories or literary tomes like Donna Tartt's *The Goldfinch*, think nothing of writing well over one hundred thousand words. The bigger the better? (Clients have brought me books for editing that weigh in at well over two hundred thousand words!) To the authors' dismay, they discover that their stories are nearly unmarketable. They have only two realistic options. Either make two (or more) novels from the one manuscript or self-publish.

Again, I encourage you to do at least a little planning before writing. I promise, you'll still have lots of room for bursts of creativity. You can pack an amazingly rich tale into eighty thousand words.

### *Yet Another Argument for Planning—Your Reader*

Most of us who write fiction for publication have two audiences: ourselves and our readers. (Although one of my friends claims she imagines her sister as her sole reader, and writes everything with Sis in mind.) If we assume that we're writing the kind of story that we might enjoy reading, then it makes sense to also consider the tastes of our readers. Because we really do want others to read us, right?

Readers enjoy discovering at least one character with whom they can bond and travel throughout the entire story. This character will generally face a strong and compelling conflict. He wants or needs to accomplish, or possess, something. And (this is important) he will care *deeply* about the outcome of the story. In other words, his motivation is strong. There often is a sense of urgency to his quest. Lives may even be at stake!

These are the reasons why readers give a fig about what happens in your story. When we read, we worry about the central character and long to discover how things will turn out for this person. The strong, emotionally charged conflict must be important enough to carry a good deal of the book.

This character may be acting in his own best interests or on behalf of someone close to him. But the conflict works best if it's relatable to the reader. If it's not, or the character seems not to have much at stake emotionally or otherwise, there's little reason for readers to stay interested in the story.

It's interesting to consider the ways in which readers' minds work. Just as we writers constantly ask ourselves questions related to plot, characters, and settings, readers also are curious and desire answers. The one question they most frequently ask is: "What happens next?" As long as the author continues to provide fresh answers to this question, by way of interesting scenes and forward-moving narrative, the reader will continue turning pages.

But as soon as we allow the story's progress to slow down or stop—in order to show off our impressive vocabulary, lecture the reader on our latest pet cause, or take him on a self-indulgent side trip through a particularly lovely botanical garden we've just visited—the reader becomes impatient and begins flipping pages. ("But what happens next?" he cries.)

If frustrated enough, he may eventually put the book down. And a reader who fails to finish reading your first book will likely never buy another with your name on it. Literary agents and acquiring editors for publishing houses will be even harsher critics.

### The Research Trap

Occasionally, a writer explains her choice of fiction over nonfiction like this: "I hate doing research. That's why I want to write fiction. Everything can come from my imagination."

Well, maybe.

But doesn't it stand to reason that we can't make up *everything* in a story and have it be believable? Even if a novel is pure fantasy, there will be reasons for referring to the real world. And once we start revising and polishing, we'll still need to pay attention to the niceties of grammar.

No writer has such a complete store of information in their head that they never need to check facts. And those of us who base our stories on history, science and technology, distant cities, or foreign customs often must spend a good deal of time digging for information.

In fact, innocent misstatements and just plain wrong "facts" are one of the most common reasons contributing to the rejection of a book. Yes, even in fiction.

Think about it. Who are the most likely people to want to read a story based on a particular topic or era? They will be the fans and subject-matter experts who gravitate toward your book. They'll instantly catch errors and let you, and the world, know it. The same is true for editors considering your novel for publication. Careless, uninformed mistakes show a lack of professionalism and suggest to the editor that she may well find other serious problems within the manuscript.

In a business as competitive as publishing, acquiring editors have a vast choice of whom to work with. Doesn't it make sense that this professional will choose an author who produces material as close as possible to publication quality? A manuscript that has fewer problems to be dealt with in-house?

So the question often arises—how does a writer know when he has done *enough* research? In other words, when can he assume he's done due diligence and now is ready to write?

The answer is, *sooner than you might think.*

Research is another of those author traps that are incredibly easy to fall into. We get sucked into our reference materials as if they are a black hole, then feel helpless to pull ourselves out of it. There's always something more to learn. Each time we enter keywords for a search on the Internet, we find more fascinating stuff! We chase new leads and find ancillary material that, although it doesn't apply to the current novel, might well be a gem to use in a future book. How can we pass it up?

And so we keep on searching.

The other tempting element of research is that it is so much *easier* to read another author's writing than it is to create original material. Someone else has sweated over these words. We're comfortable scanning documents, learning as we read, soaking up facts from a biography or letters, flipping through photographs and cool diagrams. We start to use research as an excuse to delay our own writing.

The best strategy is to begin the actual writing of a novel's draft before you think you have found everything you need to know about your subject. In general, research just long enough to feel you have enough material to launch your story with a little confidence. (e.g., you know enough to place the Eiffel Tower in the middle of Paris rather than in London. But if stating its exact height is critical to your story, you can look that up while revising.)

Remember what we said earlier in this book: Writing a novel is a lot like creating an oil painting. We work in layers. Our first layer of the book is comprised of a little thoughtful planning and research. The second layer requires creating a foundation, a rough draft. If a cool fact is nestled nicely in your head and you can pop it out and onto the page at will—fine! But if you need to stop writing and rush off to the library, or spend an hour looking up stuff online, just leave a note indicating you need to fill in that blank space later.

Something like this will do: *I need to find out how long it takes to ride on horseback between London and Glasgow.*

During revision, you'll see the message you left as a reminder and know to fill in the missing data and then make any other necessary adjustments to the text.

The key to getting quickly through a first draft is by severely limiting interruptions to your writing progress. If you stop writing every time you need to check a fact, even if it's only for thirty minutes, you may well have eaten up a third or more of your writing time for the day. And that's too dear a price to pay.

### *Keep Up the Pace*

The fact remains—*the more we write, doing it in a rapid and aggressive manner, the more fluidly our ideas will flow from our minds and onto the page.*

In addition, we've already learned that fast and focused writing silences the negative voices, helping us to make even more progress. During the draft phase, we learn our story, the parts of it we didn't know—couldn't even have guessed—when we started. And that learning process proceeds much more efficiently if we aren't gritting our teeth and trying to do everything right the first time around.

Jeffery Deaver, a consummate thriller writer, spoke at a dinner meeting of the Mid-Atlantic chapter of Mystery Writers of America . He told the group that his early drafts are no way near perfect. I think he used the term "a mess." In fact, he claimed he usually ended up completing around forty drafts before he felt the story was ready to be seen by his editor.

Whenever I feel frustrated with a story in its draft phase, I remind myself that it takes the remarkable Mr. Deaver dozens of runs at his manuscripts to bring it to the finish line.

If you promise yourself that you'll be able to return to your story again and again—each time making the writing a little stronger, the prose a little clearer, adding in more vivid details, cutting out the clutter—you'll be far less likely to view your early drafts as fatally flawed.

If the scenes you've produced on some days seem far better than on others (maybe even brilliant!), that's great. Allow yourself to bask in the glory of your accomplishments. But never let a first draft (or second or fifth) be the one that brings you crashing down, convincing you that your book isn't worth the effort, or the paper it's printed on. Remind yourself of the many glorious opportunities you have for making it everything you've ever wanted it to be.

If it takes forty drafts, so be it.

*Drafts are supposed to be messy. But out of the chaos come the most delicious stories.*

### *Ideas: Ditch the Stale, Generate Fresh*

Do you feel overwhelmed by the task of coming up with a sparkly new idea to make your story stand out from the crowd? It's often been said there are no new stories. Every possible plot device, interesting twist, or character type has been built into hundreds, if not thousands, of stories before ours.

We have to stop thinking of this as a handicap. Instead, we should embrace the oh-so-comfortable knowledge that we don't have to be intellectual giants and innovators to write a really great novel. We can be inspired by, or even outright *steal*, concepts and plot elements from published material. (How shocking!)

"But I don't want to copy another author's work!" you say. "Isn't that called plagiarism?"

No, it's not.

Legally, *ideas* can't be copyrighted. That's because ideas, whether daydreams or nightmares, are free to any human brain that seizes upon them.

# THE EXTREME NOVELIST

Just because Tom Clancy wrote what has come to be thought of as the first techno-thriller, doesn't mean others can't write books in a similar style or about the same subject. *The Hunt for Red October* crammed more than most people would ever want to know about submarines into a novel, and became a runaway bestseller. You can write a submarine story too, if you like. Reusing, reshaping, modernizing, or tweaking other people's plots or themes is an accepted way to learn our craft and even improve upon it.

But what about stories that have been done, done, and done? How can anyone make these stories fresh and truly their own? What about, say, vampires? Hundreds of tales feature these fanged, immortal creatures. Bram Stoker first conceived of using the vampire legend to fuel terrifying fiction starring these blood-sucking fiends of the night.

Authors who follow in Stoker's footsteps constantly change the rules in creative and interesting ways. Anne Rice made her vampires into protagonists who have decidedly human concerns. Vampires devised by other authors often don't worry about exposure to sunlight—it's not an issue for them. The creatures in Karen Russell's delightful short story "Vampires in the Lemon Grove," (in the book by the same name) suck lemons to take away their lust for blood. Charlaine Harris's wildly popular Sookie Stackhouse series injected humor into the dark legends. The fact is, there are unlimited ways we can massage a plot or character to make it uniquely ours.

Veteran authors know that the real question isn't *finding* an idea—it's choosing from among the endless possibilities all around them. They've learned that there will never be enough time in their lives to write all of the stories they imagine. The real issue is sorting through this amazing flood of information to find a few gems that strike an emotional chord in them.

How do we become the type of writer who always has a warehouse chock-full of enticing ideas? *We open our eyes and pay attention to both the larger universe and our own personal world.*

Let's again compare writing fiction to creating a painting. Just as the still-life artist paints his vision of an apple, which may not even look like an apple to someone else, we interpret and then write about reality through our own experiences and vision. Writers who open themselves up to their surroundings begin to view everything—their family and friends; headlines on the six o'clock news; their workplace, hobbies, and daily lives—as raw story material. It's the way in which we see the world around us, evolving from our personal history, that colors our stories, making our plots and paper people wonderfully distinctive and realistic.

### *Unique, That's You!*

Each author has a collection of one-off experiences throughout childhood, their youth, into adulthood, and (if we've lived long enough) through retirement years. These experiences become the pigments with which we will paint every story we write. We see through eyes, and feel through emotions, that are as individual as snowflakes. We couldn't write exactly the same story as another author if we tried. (Unless we actually sat down and typed, word for word, the pages from another author's book. And that *is* plagiarism.)

It takes conscious effort and intent to commit a fraud against readers and fellow authors by usurping their prose. But "borrowing" an idea is a perfectly legitimate technique. Mr. William Shakespeare did it! Every one of his plays has an origin in another writer's work, and often in historical record as well. What's good enough for Will is good enough for me, and for thousands of other authors.

When I wrote *The Gentleman Poet*, I based it on Shakespeare's famous play "The Tempest," paired with a true account of a shipwreck in 1609, which supposedly inspired the master to write his play. Some of my novel's characters evolved from the passengers' names and their jobs as listed on the actual ship's manifest. Their personalities are based on information in a letter that was sent back to England a year after the wreck when the surviving passengers finally arrived in Virginia. But what these people actually said, and how they interacted with one another, is pure speculation. Fiction! Because we just have no way of knowing, do we?

The savvy author will see the world through the eyes of an artist, soaking up details, noticing the way people react to real-life situations, paying attention to exciting or frightening events happening in the world today or recorded in history. All of this is available to any observant person, and provides compost for hundreds of stories, made fresh and believable through the individual writer's own background and experiences.

# THE EXTREME NOVELIST

Do you have to be a genius, earn an advanced degree, or live a sophisticated lifestyle to write a good novel?

No. No. *No!*

Traveling to exotic lands, partaking in clever cocktail repartee with famous people, or being young and beautiful has nothing to do with writing great fiction. If you can make your characters human, sympathetic, and believable, enabling readers to care about and bond with them—you'll attract a large and loyal following.

Author Robert James Waller did just that with his 1992 debut novel, *The Bridges of Madison County,* which became a national bestseller and, later, a movie. The story was set in rural America with a limited cast of extraordinarily ordinary (if that's possible) characters. Most notably, a farmer's wife and an itinerant photographer. The settings, too, were limited. It was the simple, human emotions in this bittersweet love story that gripped readers. They easily identified with the hero and heroine. If the setting and situations depicted on the pages lacked sophistication, so what?

*If you can make your reader care passionately about, worry over, and cheer on at least one character in your novel—you will have a fan for life.*

Look to the world closest to you, instead of at the lives of people who live in mansions, cruise the world on private yachts, or gamble away millions at posh casinos. Soak up the familiar, and then, if you like, add a dash of adventure.

The married couple who live next door to you, and shared their story of how they met, might have given you a wonderful scene for your work-in-progress. The way you felt when your childhood friend suddenly snubbed you in the school hallway will clue you in to the emotional trauma of one of your young characters.

Don't be afraid to build heartbreaking realism into your characters, based on what *you* have personally experienced. It requires opening your heart to the world, and that can be hard. But it's the honest author who isn't afraid to dig deep into the essence of what makes us human.

Writers are often told to "write what you know." As we've seen, that certainly applies to building believable, emotion-based characters. But it's also good advice when fleshing out characters' careers, geographical locations for the story, or technical aspects. If you have a little experience or you're an expert in a particular field, consider using this knowledge in some way to enrich your stories.

### *Prime Your Imagination with Facts*

Sometimes it works just as well to write what you would *like* to know. Are you aching with curiosity to see what happens in a courtroom during a trial, and think you might like to use such a scene in your novel? Sit in on some trials. Or interview a trial attorney.

I wanted to include a police dog in a mystery novel for kids but knew nothing about how handlers worked with their dogs, or what the animals were capable of. I found a nearby training facility for police dogs and arranged to observe and interview one of the trainers. The experience generated accurate and believable scenes in the story.

One of my writing friends wrote a scene in her novel that involved characters scaling a dangerously high cliff in the dark of night. The scene wasn't working at all. The character performing this difficult feat had no experience with such a demanding physical undertaking, and the author's description of the adventure lacked realism. When I suggested she needed to do a little more research on the types of gear and how it might feel for a novice to climb a sheer rock face, she took me literally. She signed up for rock-climbing lessons with a pro. The rewrite of the scene blew me away, in a good way.

Everyone has stories inside of them; we simply have to recognize that they're there and ripe for harvesting. Use your areas of expertise and stockpile of personal experiences. Supplement all of that with a little painless research into something that excites you and provides enriching material.

Loads of information exists online today. If you search for twenty minutes, you'll most likely find much of what you need as well as the name of a nearby expert who will be thrilled to share some of the finer points of what they do for a living. If you can't get out and meet face to face with an expert, check out the pro's Facebook page, blog, or website. Search for instructive videos on YouTube.

Story material all but shouts at us: "Use me! Write about me!"

Take time to sit down and make a list of what you already know. Then write down topics you'd like to learn more about.

It doesn't matter how mundane these interests might seem to you. Someone reading your story will think your career, hobby, or life event is new to them, intriguing, and maybe even exotic! But best of all, when inserted into a story, these details will feel *real*.

### *Why Your Story Needs a Powerful Opening*

All readers shop for their next novel in pretty much the same way. First, they check out the front cover and title of the novel. If these look appealing, they flip to the back cover and read the blurb that describes the story. If there are reviews, they may check these out. Still interested? Finally, they test-read the first few pages.

This last opportunity for engagement often is the only one we writers have total control over. Cover art, title, back-cover copy— these are usually handled (or manhandled) by the publisher. (If you're self-publishing, you definitely have more say in the physical appearance of the book.) But for an author who is unknown to the public, the first page of her novel is her trump card.

Think of it this way. We get this one chance, at the very outset of our novel, to entice readers into the story. What happens on page twenty isn't what sells a book. That scene you wrote in chapter 7— the one you absolutely *love* and you're sure will knock the socks off readers—won't get your book into their online shopping cart.

You must seize your reader's attention on the first page. If you're really, really good, you'll do it in the first paragraph. Maybe even in the first sentence.

Why should we have to place so much importance on openings? Isn't the promise of a great story enough?

*Absolutely not.*

As book authors we are competing with many other forms of entertainment. Unless a potential buyer sees a compelling reason for devoting precious time to reading what you have to say, she won't check your book out of the library, or plunk down cash on the bookstore counter, or download it. Your novel needs to stand out. It must convince this reader to move past the first sentence, down the first page, continue through the first chapter, and keep on reading.

Our jet-paced, twenty-first-century lifestyle, and increasing reliance on visual images, have influenced our reading habits. This trend is irreversible. Few adults today have the luxury of uninterrupted hours in which to spend reading for pure pleasure. We are forced to seize our leisure time where we can.

We read on our lunch hour, while commuting on the subway or waiting for a bus. We read on a tablet or even on a cell phone. People who spend a lot of time commuting by car, or driving as part of their jobs, often enjoy audio books (the old "books-on-tape") as a solution to shortened conventional reading times. The voice of a professional reader wafts from the vehicle's speakers, or through earbuds or noise-reducing earphones wherever the book lover happens to be.

All of these modern forms of reading affect the way writers write. (Arguably, they *should* alter the way we write.) Some authors tweak their writing styles by creating shorter, tighter sentences and briefer chapters because these better suit the small screens on which many people read today. Other authors keep to their same style but choose to use fewer dialogue tags (*he said, Delores added, I screamed*) because these clutter the dramatic performance in audio formats. The great thing about having these reading devices is that they make it easier for *more* people to spend *more* time with your books.

But there's a downside.

That same tablet on which much of your potential audience stores their electronic books also offers up movies and games, and can stream sporting events. Readers have almost unlimited choices these days when feeding their hunger for stories. It's because we are competing for our audience's time that we need, more now than ever, to immediately draw in our readers. We can't let them become distracted by other opportunities for entertainment. We need to make our story—irrespective of genre—irresistible from the get-go.

How do we do this?

### *Hook Your Reader*

The opening few sentences of your novel must grab your readers' attention. Make them so curious that they feel compelled to read the next paragraph, and the next one after that. One of the easiest ways to do this is by providing a vivid, active scene in which one or more of your central characters appears. This scene will also define the sort of story you're about to tell.

# THE EXTREME NOVELIST

This incredibly effective means of pulling readers into a story is called *The Hook*—a term the publishing industry borrowed from Hollywood. Filmmakers, literary agents, and acquiring editors at publishing houses demand a hook of some sort. So do readers, although they may not recognize it by name.

When someone cracks open your book and sample-reads the first page, they are asking you, "So, author, what do you have to offer me? Why should I devote precious hours out of my hellishly busy week to read your story?"

The most successful authors are often those who recognize the nature of a good hook. Here are just a few of my favorite opening lines from published novels:

"My mother did not tell me they were coming." Tracy Chevalier, *Girl with a Pearl Earring*

"If Jermyn Edmondson, the marquess of Northcliff, had known he was about to be kidnapped, he wouldn't have gone out on a walk." Christina Dodd, *The Barefoot Princess*

"There is no end of things in the heart." Michael Connelly, *Lost Light*

"One. Two. Three. How many bells? Half-Tom the dwarf huffed his way to Norwich market, squinting at the sun overhead and counting." Brenda Rickman Vantrease, *The Illuminator*

"It seemed like a good idea at the time." Laura Lippman, *The Last Place*

"The last camel died at noon." Ken Follett, *The Key to Rebecca*

Notice that in each of these samples, something about the story's genre, writing style, or tone is revealed. Some excerpts actually add visual elements. We also sense a subtle, or strong, tension, which works to propel the reader further into the book. Think about what each opening does for that particular story.

Chevalier's opening hints at mysterious visitors. We want to read on to find out why the narrator sounds anxious. And, by the way, why did her mother keep from her the fact "they" were coming?

Dodd suggests treachery is about to happen. We don't yet know the marquess, but we are nevertheless curious to see how his kidnapping comes about and whether he'll be harmed.

Connelly connects with his readers through universal human emotion. We wonder—will this be a love story? A tale of family loyalty or tragedy? No real action yet, but the passion is there, and that's enough as long as he gets things moving soon. And he does.

Vantrease pulls us into an active scene that we already sense verges on urgency. We feel compassion for this "half-man" whose name indicates his community pokes fun at him for being different. A man who also appears to be late for an important event, and worried about the time. As a bonus, the author tips us off, through her word choices, that this will be historical fiction.

Lippman uses her opening to warn us that something has gone wrong. Did this misstep result in dire consequences? Who *cannot* read on to find out what that is?

Follett loads a ton of information and questions into a six-word sentence. If camels are involved, we must be in the desert. If they are dying, there's no water, and whatever humans may be with them probably are close to death, as well as without transportation.

The hook technique requires that the author respect the reader's desire to dive immediately into an absorbing story. If we delay the real opening of our tale with a lot of preparatory information, this sends a message to the reader that he is expected to remember these factoids. Reading then begins to look a lot like work.

Our job as novelists, more than anything else, is to entertain. If we intend to teach readers something along the way, we are better off doing it subtly, within the deeper reaches of our story. Not on page one. Never as a lecture or rant.

As writers we're often tempted to include what's called "backstory" in a preface or first chapter of a novel. This is information we sometimes believe the reader needs to know, to understand our characters or set up the story we're about to tell. It may include such details as facts about a character's earlier life, the history of the town in which the story takes place, or technical information.

Editors call this an "information dump." It's obvious this isn't meant as praise. Whatever information is important to understanding the story or its characters can be revealed later. (Remember, there will be hundreds of pages to fill!)

Much of the enjoyment in reading book-length fiction comes from being dropped into the middle of a moment in a character's life. Slowly, we begin to discover what makes him tick and what's going on. As we dig out little nuggets of information throughout the novel, we begin to piece together the puzzle of sorts. And that's a great deal of the fun in reading fiction. Taking that joy of discovery away from the reader with an information dump is like giving away the punch line of a great joke. It's just poor timing.

### *Start with an Instigating Moment*

Instead of slowly warming up to a story with information the reader doesn't really need (character sketches, historical essays, a weather report or lovely sunset) determine the instigating moment that sets your plot in action. This is an incident in the main character's life when things take a critical turn, sometimes spinning his world out of control.

An instigating moment is active and visible, and almost always is placed close to the beginning of your novel. It is an incident that will alter your central character's life in some meaningful way. He must respond to this event—which may take the form of a threat, a challenge, a notable life-event, or an emotional realization. The incident is even more traumatic if the character senses there's no turning back to his former situation. He must choose a direction, deal with the situation one way or another.

How do we choose just the *right* moment with which to begin the story? After all, there are endless possibilities for starting points, aren't there? We know now that it's a good idea to launch with a hook that tweaks readers' curiosity. A scene or statement that intrigues and draws the reader into our narrative and, hopefully, encourages our audience to trust us as a storyteller.

If you've already sketched out a synopsis, or overview, of your story, you'll have a rough blueprint to work from. That's good. Now think about your story as if each scene were a domino tile. When you were a kid did you set up a boxful of dominoes, placing each one on end in a long, serpentine pattern? The fun was in clicking over the first domino and then watching them fall, one at a time, in a glorious, clattering chain reaction.

This is what we are aiming for as we assess an opening scene. It is as if this scene is the first domino, which will trigger a human chain reaction. This initial scene sets the story in motion. Without that first critical event, the rest of the story might not even have happened. In some stories, the climax and resolution may appear (in hindsight) almost inevitable.

When I was working on one of my historical novels, *The Gentleman Poet*, I was troubled by the question of where to begin. My heroine is the daughter of an apothecary with a thriving business in seventeenth-century London. Her family is well placed in the emerging merchant class. But she will find her circumstances reversed, reducing her to the role of an orphaned serving girl and a passenger on a ship bound for Jamestown, Virginia. That's largely where I wanted most of the drama to take place, on that voyage, which ends up taking a full year.

So where should I begin? I could start with Elizabeth and her family in London during happier times. That would establish her background and enable lots of interesting scenes. I could show the tension between religious factions of the time, which result in terror, violence, and the execution of those who happen to practice the "wrong" religion. I might have shown the horrors of a city held hostage by the Black Plague, which decimated entire populations. Both religion and disease have a role in destroying the family Elizabeth loved, leaving her destitute, forced into servitude. But would these scenes have launched the story at the most effective time, given my vision of the story?

Ultimately, the answer is *no*. Elizabeth's literary journey needed to start at the *instigating moment*, that is, at the point in time when, for her, there is no turning back. Unable to control her own destiny, she must depend upon her mistress's whims and go where the old woman takes her. And so the book begins onboard the *Sea Venture*, sailing into a storm at sea, when all aboard fear for their lives and it is uncertain whether the ship will stay afloat long enough for them to reach land.

The tension is immediate because of the life-or-death situation. Yes, readers eventually will need to know how Elizabeth came, unwillingly, to be on this ship. Yes, they'll want to learn what happened to her family. But all of that backstory can wait until their interest has been secured and the story is underway. Then the details of her personal history can be woven into the remainder of the story, revealed naturally through her dialogue and thoughts.

This gradual revelation of facts feeds readers' curiosity, their "need to know." Weaving information bit by bit through the story guarantees your audience will want to keep turning pages. If I had dumped Elizabeth's history at the front of the book, the reader might well have felt overwhelmed. And my heroine would be less of a mystery.

Return to books that you've loved, with which you immediately felt a connection. You'll likely find that the author (perhaps quite consciously) created a sense of tension, subtle or so obvious you couldn't miss it, somewhere within the initial chapter. In particular, look to books that have been published in the past three or four years. They will provide the best models of current style.

Of course we love our classics and return to them over and over again for reading pleasure. But some older novels take considerable time to "get into." For readers of a hundred (or even fewer) years ago, who had no television, movies, or videos to set a rapid pace for their imaginations, a delightfully leisurely or fact-packed opening might have worked. These readers had the patience to follow the author's lead and trust the story would eventually arrive at some place that was interesting to them.

Our twenty-first-century readers are far less forgiving. Sad to say, we've been programmed for immediate gratification.

The good news is this: a fast start, with an instigating moment, is a tool we can consciously make work for us. Moreover, this technique applies to virtually all genres, including literary and experimental fiction.

Consider Donna Tartt's acclaimed, prize-winning literary novel *The Goldfinch*. Tartt is a truly gifted writer capable of delving deeply into her characters and bringing them to life for her readers. She's a wordsmith whose writing evokes rich images. She can wax poetic on a single artist or painting within a museum, and string us along for a page or more.

But she also uses every trick in the book that commercial fiction writers employ to make their scenes come to life and connect with the reader through emotion. We feel a powerful connection with the troubled young boy, her main character, who grows toward manhood throughout this story. She borrows genre fiction tropes: child in jeopardy, art theft, terrorism, chase scenes, and more. But she enriches her novel with universal themes, such as the vulnerability of human beings to chaos.

In short, she makes us feel we are right there, in the story, watching it all happen. *She creates a movie in the reader's head!*

## Chapter 6: Connect Reader & Character

In the last chapter we learned about the importance of creating a hook to provide a strong beginning for our novel and entice the reader to enter into our adventure and keep turning pages.

Is this manipulating readers?

*Absolutely.*

Is this unfair?

*Not at all.*

When we write fiction, we are attempting to connect with our readers' emotional and intellectual need for a good story. To feel compelled to read our fiction, readers must first *feel* something. That something can be admiration, fear, curiosity, joy, horror, or any number of other emotions. What we as writers must avoid is allowing our audience to sink into indifference. Readers have to care deeply about, and be interested in, at least one central character in the story, or they stop reading.

Creating this caring link between reader and character takes planning. But it is well worth the effort. If this connection is made early in the novel, there's a better chance of fully engaging your reader.

### *Make a Promise*

The savvy author makes a unspoken pact with her audience at the start of each novel. Through her choice of words, tone, and subject matter in the opening scenes, she promises: *This is the kind of story I'm going to tell. If this sounds interesting to you, stick around. You'll be rewarded.*

Thus, if you open your story with a light-hearted incident, humorous characters, and a gentle mystery, readers will know that you're writing what's called a "cozy." Fans of this type of mystery know that the tale won't involve bloodletting or sex on the page. They will have a pleasant, safe adventure. There likely will be an interesting puzzle to be solved, the bad guys will be punished, and all will be right in the world by the last page. A cozy author knows not to introduce an ax murderer lopping off limbs in the middle of the book. This would break the promise she made to her readers, and she would surely lose them.

Likewise, the reader looking for a truly chilling horror story will know, after checking out the opening pages of a novel, that the novel described above isn't for her. She'll look elsewhere for dark thrills.

If every novel you write fulfills its opening promises to readers, and you return time and again to this genre and style, these same readers will eagerly reach for more of your books. They liked what they saw the first time, and now they want more. In addition, they will talk up your novels to friends who share their reading tastes.

Uber-popular authors like John Green, Nora Roberts, and Stephen King have learned this lesson well. When readers pick up their books they know from their earlier reading experience (as well as from reviews) exactly what they're going to get in exchange for their dollars and time.

Green delivers highly emotional young-adult drama that even adult readers can't put down. He has an aggressive following ready to snap up his next book even before it hits bookstores or online vendors, as evidenced by prepublication sales.

Nora Roberts's fans travel across state lines and hundreds of miles when her appearances are announced, just to see her, buy her latest novel, and have her sign their books.

Stephen King's body of work has defined horror. He's also known for his lucid and compelling writing, and for his advocacy of quality prose. (If you can only afford one how-to book on writing fiction, you might be wise to make it Stephen King's *On Writing*.) Everyone knows when we pick up one of King's books what sort of story it will be. Sometime before the end, things are going to get spooky, scary, and probably pretty bloody.

Is this typecasting of sorts? Maybe. In the publishing world it's referred to as "branding." But that's not a bad thing because it works to an author's advantage. Usually. Nora Roberts is known for her romances. But when she wanted to write something other than the particular type of story she'd become famous for, she needed to create a new persona for herself: J. D. Robb. Fans of Robb know to expect a crime story set in the near future, something closer to a police procedural than a romance.

If you're an author working on your debut novel (a term for the first of your novels to be published, not necessarily the first you write), then ask yourself what sort of story will this be? Is this the kind of tale you'll be happy writing more of in the future? Because if you sell this book and readers respond positively to it, they (and your publisher) will expect you to write more of the same.

They'll also want to know how soon they can put their hands on your next book. So you might want to start thinking about ways to write faster...*which is sort of the point of this book!*

### *Introduce Conflict ASAP*

Let's take discussion of your story's opening even further.

Not only will you reveal to the reader the type of story you'll be telling, you will let the reader in on the central conflict and the protagonist's goal. This may be the same as your hook, or it may mean something different.

It's best to reveal the main conflict very early in the story, regardless of the genre. By doing so you are presenting to your reader a set of ground rules for the game that's about to be played.

This is quite literally done by Suzanne Collins, author of the runaway bestseller *The Hunger Games*. We learn in the very first chapter that children and teenagers in a dystopian culture are being forced to fight to the death. Even more shocking, the heroine will be one of the combatants; she has volunteered to save her younger sister from almost certain death.

When you give the reader enough information to know the type of journey they will be taking, it increases interest. Your audience, in effect, signs on for the adventure and becomes a willing accomplice.

"But," you say, "if I tell the reader what to expect, isn't that giving away valuable information? Isn't that wasting surprises that should be saved for later in the story?"

Most of the time, no.

Readers will want to go along for the ride because of their need to know what's going to happen. Will the main character succeed in reaching her goal? Will this person I've learned to care about even survive to the end of the tale?

73

You can still hold back plenty of information, and provide loads of clever twists and turns in your plot. Readers will look forward to experiencing these along the way. It's this pattern of gradually fulfilling the reader's need for a great story, and a satisfying resolution, that will keep him reading to the very end of your book.

As an example, your underlying message to readers might be: "This is going to be an amazing military thriller featuring a main character who will place himself in harm's way to save others. There will be car chases, assorted weaponry and gunplay, considerable danger, and violence. Stick with me and find out whether the good guys survive and make the bad guys pay for their evildoings." (Authors like Lee Child, Harlan Coben, and Tess Gerritsen have built careers on this style of fiction.)

Another novel's opening scenes might telegraph a completely different message to readers: "This will be a love story about two people struggling to blend their lives in today's challenging world, with the hope of marriage and creating a family. Trust me—you *won't* encounter graphic violence and there *will* be a happily-ever-after ending." (Think: Brenda Novak, Debbie Macomber, or Susan Wiggs.)

If you write science-fiction epics, you may promise your readers something along the lines of: "Prepare yourself for adventuring into distant universes in a future where the technology will be mind blowing. You'll meet aliens, good and bad, and experience what it might be like to travel through space."

By providing up-front scenes that demonstrate genre and style, you are asking your audience to trust you with their time and emotions. Once readers trust you as a reliable storyteller, they are more likely to accept your characters and story as believable. That leap of faith from our audience is what we're striving for as storytellers.

In *Wired for Story* by Lisa Cron, the author suggests that the human brain is geared to accept stories as a means of gathering information and learning. She also proposes that the most effective way of reaching out to a reader is often through fiction that connects reader and characters through the universal emotions we all share. I highly recommend this book to any writer who wants to better understand how to grab and hold their audience's attention.

# THE EXTREME NOVELIST

### *Create a Movie in Your Reader's Head*

If you've read articles or books about the craft of fiction, you've undoubtedly heard the advice: "Show, Don't Tell." In fact it's repeated so often that these words tend to become white noise in the background of our brains. How can we escape from the need to narrate (telling) when that's what we naturally *do* when relating a story? Don't we always say we're *telling* a story?

Novelists are not journalists, whose job is to report only the facts and describe incidents in a detached manner. Rather, the fiction author's goal is to help the reader envision the story as it spills out across the page and connect emotionally with what's happening. In essence we want to create images as close as possible to those the moviegoer sees in a theater. We play our images across a screen that exists in the reader's mind.

Why is this so much better than just letting a story flow through narration alone?

Imagine, if you will, buying a ticket to see a play. You're very excited about this performance. Perhaps a veteran actor you've always admired has the lead role. So you pay a premium price for an orchestra seat as close to the stage as possible. You'll be able to see every gesture, hear every whisper from the actors. You're ready for a wonderful performance.

Sitting in your seat, you turn your full attention to the stage as the action begins and the performance starts. The characters on stage speak to one another, shout or weep or laugh when appropriate. They move across the stage, handling props and gesturing as they deliver their lines, and the drama becomes increasingly exciting and powerful.

Just when you're literally on the edge of your seat, the curtain drops, and a man steps in front of it and faces the audience. He says: "And now Frederick and Marilyn argue. He flies into a rage and strikes her so hard that she falls to the floor. Stunned, she is unable to get up for many minutes. The next day, when guests show up at the house, Marilyn is nervous around her husband, but he pretends nothing has happened. For days after that neither of them speak of the incident..."

By now you are no longer enjoying the drama. This intermediary (the narrator) has come between you and the characters you care about. Sure, he's conveying what is happening, but you're unable to *witness* the action firsthand. You are no longer a participant, not even vicariously. You feel frustrated, cheated. You may even end up walking out of the theater at intermission.

Narration can be an important element of a story. We do need it. But we have other options for delivering information to readers. If, as the author, we're given the choice between narrating a scene or using a blend of the characters' dialogue, actions, thoughts, and emotional reactions—doesn't it make sense to choose the method that creates the most realistic and vivid image in the reader's mind?

### *Choose Universal Emotions*

To say that all human beings share similar emotions sounds like a no-brainer. Of course we all fear something. Of course love, hate, a sense of self-worth are all feelings we experience. So what? How does this impact the success of the fiction we write?

As author Lisa Cron explains, these shared emotions are the reason an American reader of twenty-first-century literature can identify with, and care about, a merchant in sixteenth-century Italy, an Icelandic cave dweller, or a child growing up in sub-Saharan Africa. Time and distance fail to alter our common needs, desires, and concerns.

We work hard to provide shelter for ourselves and our loved ones. We worry about having enough of the right kind of food to stay healthy. We love our children and try to protect them. Most of us will avoid physical danger, knowing that if we take too many chances we are likely to shorten our life or inflict pain on ourselves. We fear death.

Furthermore, unless an individual is emotionally crippled in some way (e.g., suffers from a form of autism or a brain injury), he will be able to sympathize with other human beings (and even nonhuman creatures) who find themselves in challenging and, especially, in life-threatening situations.

So when a character in a story reacts in a highly emotional way to a specific need or desire, the reader who cares about this character will experience a taste of that same emotion. This frisson of emotion creates tension in the reader and spurs him to read on, because he is truly concerned and wants to see how things will turn out for the story character.

Therefore, it follows that if we want readers to emotionally bond with one or more of our paper people, we would be well advised to convey the urgency of the character's dilemma and need to succeed, as well as the strength of his emotional reaction. How do we do that?

### *Name the Desperately Sought Goal*

First we have to ask ourselves one important question: *What does my character desperately want or need?*

In other words, what does your character believe he or she must achieve or possess by the end of the story? Once we know that answer, move on to the next question: *What will happen if my character is unable to get what he/she wants?*

In other words, what is the cost of failure?

If, for instance, your protagonist can simply return to the status quo, to life as it was (which, perhaps, wasn't all that bad), then the tension and the author's ability to show the story in a way that will hold readers' interest are weakened. After all, our goal is to establish and then sustain tension between characters throughout the entire story. Once the tension leaves entirely, the story is over.

Let's think a little more about this. Imagine a character is trying to solve a murder mystery. You've set things up so there's a clear possibility he might not succeed. That automatically creates tension. Great! But if he has the option of dropping that case and moving on to another one that promises to be easier to solve, and there are no negative consequences for his having failed to close the initial case, then it's clear to the reader there was never much at stake.

The tension meter drops to zero.

Or perhaps, in an attempt to woo a young woman, our hero tries dating her by bringing her flowers and laying his heart on the line. He confesses he loves her, but she spurns him and walks away from the relationship. He may be heartbroken. At that horrible moment of rejection, he may even feel his life is over. But what is to keep him from simply setting his sights on another pretty gal? If we don't provide convincing need and emotional motivation for our hero, the reader may think the character doesn't ring true. He's obsessing over this woman for no logical reason.

Conflict and tension are intimately tied to the importance we give to a character's particular desire or need. It is this *importance* that the reader must feel in order to buy into the story. It's the author's job to show his reader the cost of failure. And it must be a high cost to count for anything. Failure that warrants a shrug and a *c'est la vie* isn't strong enough to support a novel.

Success, too, can have risks and a cost. We can point these out to readers as well.

Nancy may get the job she's competed for and deserves. But if her best friend also had hoped to get the same job, their friendship may have been destroyed by their rivalry.

Clive might rescue his child from the burning house but be unable to return to it for his wife, who perishes in the blaze.

A lone cowboy fends off a gang of gunslingers and protects his hometown but is so gravely injured in the fight he'll never ride the range again.

Ask yourself why it is critical that your character succeeds. What is really at stake here? Will the hero or heroine suffer irreparable loss of pride or reputation? Is this struggle a matter of life or death? Why is success crucial? What stops the character from simply returning to the status quo and going on with life as it was before?

Without conflict, it has been said, there is no story. Characters who are content with their present circumstances, or agree with one another about virtually everything, are not only uninteresting they are unlifelike. Put two people together in a room in real life, and there is bound to be conflict on some level. This tension may be subtle, each of them thinking about what to say to the other, or what they want out of this meeting or relationship. But conflict of some kind is almost always at work.

Think about your extended family. If they all meet up for a picnic or holiday event is the day destined to be tranquil and pleasant? Will there be no arguments? No hard feelings, backbiting, displays of jealousy or pettiness by the end of the day? I'd venture to say that emotion will play a role, one way or another.

This is why emotion is, in so many ways, the writer's most powerful tool for creating believable, rich, and compelling characters. If we use it effectively, we'll never lack for avid readers.

## Chapter 7: Characters

The literary agent had just met with one of my students at a local writer's conference. She had reviewed the opening pages of his novel, and I was eager to hear her opinion. I knew Marvin was hopeful of securing an agent to represent his book to major publishers—the kind of publishers impossible to approach without representation. He'd already submitted query letters and sample chapters to more than a dozen agents but hadn't gotten as much as a nibble.

"Ah, yes, Marvin's story," she said. "I loved his voice and, of course, his use of language. Unfortunately, after reading a little more than the first chapter, I had to tell him it wasn't right for me at this time." The typical nonhelpful response many writers get from agents.

"Can you tell me why you didn't ask to see the rest of the book?" I nudged.

She thought for a moment. "I rejected the manuscript because I couldn't figure out who the protagonist was. There were just so many characters knocking about in the book. I honestly had trouble connecting with any one of them."

I've heard similar objections from other agents and acquiring editors. This problem of lack of focus and character overload (or underdevelopment) has deep-sixed many a novel with otherwise good writing. It breaks my heart to watch as a student's exciting concept and beautiful prose go unpublished simply because the writer didn't understand one thing: *Where characters are concerned, more is not necessarily better.*

Choosing your cast of characters is, ideally, a task the writer should tackle before beginning the writing process. Of course, one can clean up a cast of characters during the revision process, if necessary. But let's talk about your novel as if you haven't written it yet; you're just in the planning stages.

The proposed length of your novel—as well as its genre, complexity of plot, and length of time the story covers (hours, days, years?)—will contribute to the size of the novel's cast. It's possible to write an entire book with a cast of one, perhaps with a few minor supporting characters for several scenes. Sometimes these are survival tales, wherein the protagonist is trapped in an isolated setting. Daniel Defoe's *Robinson Crusoe* comes to mind.

A somewhat more recent novel for young readers, *Hatchet* by Gary Paulsen, deposits a young boy in remote woodlands after he alone survives a small-plane crash. Such a plot setup creates a challenging job for the writer, because it limits possibilities for conversation and interaction between characters. However, an advantage to having only a very few characters is the ease with which the writer can create a strong bond between reader and the main character. Without a multitude of personalities running around in the book—muddying the focus and distracting us from what the main character is trying to achieve—the reader comes to know more intimately and care more deeply about that one person: the protagonist.

In considering the cast for your novel, choose a single character *you* would most like the reader to become attached to and follow through the story. (By the way, this has nothing to do with Perspective, also called Point of View. You still may have multiple POVs throughout the novel, if that's what you want.) If you, the author, single out the individual you wish readers to sympathize with and cheer for throughout the book, and you write the story with this selection in mind, the reader will most likely do as you have suggested.

By returning repeatedly to this one character and his or her concerns, the author directs the reader's focus to the concerns and experiences of this person, so that the plot doesn't feel overly scattered to the reader.

But there's another reason for making one of your characters a "star." It has to do with why we read novels at all. We enjoy getting close to and observing the life of another person for what that experience can teach us about our own lives. When we read fiction, we fall a little in love with, admire, are fascinated by, or worry about a special character who is so well written that we can't help believing she is real.

Thus, as authors, if we want to keep readers engaged and turning pages, we need to encourage a bond between the reader and a lead character, then keep this person in the forefront much of the time.

This is more easily done with fewer distractions—such as a dozen other characters competing for our attention, taking turns at stealing the show by telling their own stories. Equally damaging is a long string of scenes in which our main character either doesn't appear at all or fails to have an active role.

Not long ago, I was reading the manuscript of a very talented writer in preparation for writing a critique for her. I was pleased to see her protagonist taking firm charge of the opening three chapters. This was a gripping historical mystery. The author had done a great job of getting me involved with the male sleuth from the get-go. I was ready to stay up all night reading the manuscript, it was that fascinating!

However, at around page forty-five the author suddenly shifted gears to a female character's point of view and a totally different setting. At first I wasn't too concerned; these scenes were interesting, too. I kept on reading, trusting that the author would soon bring me back to the character I'd so loved and labeled "protagonist." But the scenes involving this new character continued for nearly another fifty pages. I completely lost track of the original character, even though I still hoped that the two plot lines might eventually converge. However, the gap proved too long. After I'd read another ten pages, the "hero" still hadn't returned.

*What's up with that?* I thought, feeling utterly frustrated. After all, wasn't he the star of the show? Where had he gone?

As it turned out, when I asked the author which of her characters she considered her lead, she told me it was most definitely the female. The sleuth had just seemed like a more interesting way to start the book and introduce the mystery as well as important backstory.

This sort of imbalance of character representation is a serious problem because readers often assume that the first character they see, or hear speak, will be the one they are meant to follow through the story. Or, as in this case, the sleuth will at least be really, really important to the novel. This level of importance is reinforced when the character holds forth for more than a few pages. If, after dozens of pages, it turns out this first-appearing character isn't the star of the show, the reader may feel misled and confused (like me), and suspect a lack of control on the author's part. At which point the reader stops trusting the story as well as the storyteller. Chances are he may even give up on the book. Just as that literary agent did.

There's another reason why one needs to plan openings carefully. That is: publishing goals. This particular author was determined to secure a literary agent and a traditional New York publishing house for her book. One of the so-called Big Five. But an acquiring editor at a major house like Simon & Schuster or HarperCollins would likely view the structure of this novel as problematic. And because correcting this issue would require a great deal of work on the part of the editor, coaching the author through the process of revisions, the novel was doomed to rejection unless the author rectified the situation.

An author who sees his novel as a grand and glorious production with a sprawling cast of characters, or even an ensemble cast, may have a wonderful story to tell and the skills with which to pull it off. Or he may have bitten off more than he can chew or his readers can swallow. Few books today are published on the scale of *War and Peace*. Instead, agents and publishers hunt for fiction that beckons readers into the lives and minds of just a few characters.

This is a fact that many best-selling authors have learned. *A limited cast, focused on one or two lead characters who are emotionally entangled in a plot of some urgency, is guaranteed to draw readers.* If you can create this intimate reader-character bond, you'll have a novel that's not only hard to put down—it will be passed from hand to hand with glowing recommendations.

### *Make the Story Yours*

We've been talking about general fiction techniques and strategies for writing a rough draft of any novel. Now it's time to consider your work-in-progress. The novel *you* are most interested in writing these days.

Who is your main character? If you aren't sure, ask yourself who has the most to lose or gain when considering the outcome of your story.

Another good test question is: Which character will likely be most actively involved in the majority of scenes? Characters who watch from the sidelines are less interesting and need to be demoted to secondary roles.

You do know the resolution of your story, don't you? I don't mean exactly how your final scenes will play out, word for word. We're talking about the basic destination of the story. If you're still convinced that a detailed plot outline isn't for you, then at least make a few decisions around which you can structure the story.

Will the lovers end up together?

Will the killer be brought to justice?

Will the young boy and his friends escape the zombies?

Once you know the basic goal and resolution, ask yourself what your central character must risk or sacrifice in order to achieve what he/she desperately needs or wants.

If your answer falls into the "nothing all that important" category (a week's wages, his summer vacation, the new sweater she longed to buy), then this suggests you need to up the stakes and provide stronger conflict and motivation.

If you're satisfied with your source and intensity of conflict, apply it to one or more of your characters. A conflict can challenge just one person or an entire civilization. But in order for us to experience emotion, we need to see through the eyes and feel through the heart of at least one main character.

Can we get away with having two, three, or even five central characters? Yes. But the question is do they really *need* to be equally important?

A good example of the use of multiple central characters is just about any TV sitcom. Take the one-time popular show *Sex and the City*. Each episode focused on four young women who shared a close personal relationship while living and working in New York City. And yet, the viewer always understood that one stood out; she was the star. That was Carrie.

Determining ahead of time which character will play the lead enables the author to better develop scenes with an eye toward the most dramatic impact. If you have in mind that Sarabelle will be the character you wish readers to care about most deeply, then you will probably want more, if not all, scenes to be shown through her perspective. We'll be in her head more often than not.

Authors who choose a single point of view for an entire novel, never showing any scene outside of that character's experience or knowledge, know they can create an amazingly strong attachment between reader and character. Admittedly, there are some disadvantages. We can't show a scene without that character present. We can't read another character's thoughts. But the trade-off can be worth it.

The point is, staying away from a main character for too long may encourage your reader to skip over pages in search of the person and action they most care about. This sign of dissatisfaction can worsen to the point of total disengagement. At best, the reader won't finish the book. At worst, she'll heave your precious baby at the nearest wall in frustration. Not high praise for a novel.

### Use Only As Many As You Need

Given what we've just discussed, a good rule of thumb is to limit your cast of characters to those absolutely necessary to tell the story. Yes, I realize this sounds like simple common sense, but it's amazing how many authors pack in character after character until an appendix or *dramatis personae* is necessary to keep them sorted. The reader feels compelled to memorize (or keep checking) names, relationships, jobs, and backgrounds for dozens of people. This becomes hard work. All the fun is gone!

If you think you need lots of characters to fill minor roles, and each one only appears once or twice in the entire book, you might try combining jobs. Make one character do for two roles. The postal carrier who delivers an important package might also be the unfortunate person who stumbles on the body. The soldier in one scene in the training camp might also be the individual who is wounded in battle later on. The key is to beware of stuffing unnecessary characters into a narrative, when all it does is clutter scenes and drain them of focus and power.

However, there is at least one type of novel for which you may need to *add* more characters. That's one or another form of the murder mystery. Suspense tales, thrillers, detective fiction, espionage stories—all of these and their mystery subgenres need a sufficient supply of victims and suspects to hide the true identity of the perpetrator. Eventually the truth of who is behind all the nastiness will be revealed, along with motivation for why the antagonist did what he did. But enough survivors must hang around to provide a perplexing mix of possible killers.

For most novels, it's entirely up to the author to decide on the best mix of characters for his story. Whenever you introduce a new character in your story, ask yourself what significant role they will play. If they're not needed, boot them out or reduce them to walk-on roles as part of the scenery.

### Build a Lead Character Worthy of Your Reader

How, then, can we be confident that our main character is strong enough to carry the responsibility of a lead role? After all, the success of the story rests on that individual. If readers can't identify with the character, don't even like her, will they care what happens to her?

Agreed, readers have preferences where characters are concerned. We can't guarantee that everyone will adore our paper people. We can aim for a majority of readers. And we do this by giving our most important characters an appealing mix of positive and negative traits, and by making our fantasy people as human and sympathetic as possible.

Heroes and heroines may be flawed, but overall they're *good* people. We might imagine emulating them or chatting with them over dinner, if we could. Moreover they have fears, desires, needs just like ours. When they are faced with a challenge or conflict, we naturally want to see them succeed. If the consequences are dire, we hope they'll survive.

Consider the main character in your work-in-progress. Can you list his or her positive traits? Does this character have a major personality flaw or bad habit that will make him seem more human? Do you, the author, really like this character? Why? If you do, is it just because she is your creation? Or he's a mirror image of you? Can you see something special or unique about her that not only draws you to her, but is likely to interest readers?

A word about historical characters. In general, choosing a real historical figure for your lead can add an extra level of appeal for readers. But if this person is unfamiliar to most of today's readers, giving him or her the lead in your story might not be the best idea. Readers of historical fiction usually gravitate toward characters who are famous, or at least a little familiar to them.

However, giving lesser-known historical figures a secondary role can work exceptionally well, making the story seem all the more realistic. And using a fictional person as a lead often gives the author the maximum flexibility for plotting; you don't need to worry quite so much about contradicting history when you're the one who invented the character.

Ken Follett does this very effectively in many of his sprawling historical novels (such as *World Without End, Fall of Giants*, and *Winter of the World*.) His imagined characters may come into contact with, or be aware of, an assortment of historical figures during the story.

As mentioned earlier, I used a Shakespearean legend (about the writing of *The Tempest*) as the basis for one of my novels. But when I tried to follow up with another story about a seventeenth-century man of letters, John Milton, my editor rejected it. Her reasoning was that not enough readers of commercial fiction had heard of Milton to care about his story. I disagree, but it's hard to fight the gatekeepers of commercial publishing.

Creating characters that target a niche audience may sound like a good idea, and it can work. But if traditional publishers aren't enthusiastic about the project, the author may be pressed to self-publish. Which isn't necessarily a bad thing. It's just a different publishing experience. Some novels are hard sales, no matter how much we love them and how well written they are.

In the publishing world, money is the bottom line. Books are chosen not necessarily on their merit. They are accepted for publication based on projected sales. Niche novels and those inspired by memoirs, family letters, or oral history are often the toughest to pitch. To us, Grandmother's experiences coming to this country from the Old World may be wonderful stuff—after all, it's our heritage! However readers who aren't members of the author's family may find Grammy's "adventures" snoreworthy.

In short, if you wish to share your story with the world and attract the largest number of readers interested in buying your book, you might wish to aim for universal, appealing, active, emotionally charged characters who share traits most of us can identify with.

"Aha!" you say. "But what about the antihero? Can't the star of my novel be a character readers love to hate?"

Without doubt, our imaginations have been captured by characters whose evil intentions are so mesmerizing we can't tear ourselves away from them. Hannibal Lecter comes to mind.

The antihero can be a valuable tool. But is Hannibal the protagonist of Thomas Harris's *Silence of the Lambs*? No, that honor goes to the young female detective, Clarice. She is the character we come to care deeply about and cheer on throughout the novel. Lecter, the psychopath with his flesh-eating, I'll-screw-with-your-head nastiness, is critical to the story but isn't the lead.

Aside from the normal device of assigning a good guy as the lead and a bad guy as the antagonist, there's a very practical reason for not making an antihero your lead. And this is it: Unless things change in the publishing world, selling an antihero story has always been as difficult as selling a novel with a downer ending. Either one, these days, seems to be the kiss of death. (With the possible exception of Dexter, the serial killer of TV fame.)

The point is, with your writing career on the line—why make selling your book any harder than it has to be? If you can avoid including something in your novel that is going to make agents and acquiring editors cringe and run in the other direction, why do it?

If this sounds suspiciously like compromising your artistic vision—to a certain extent, it is. Sometimes we need to leverage the odds in our favor to reach our publication goals. But isn't this a lot like life in general?

## Chapter 8: It's All About Choices

Earlier in this book we said that whenever we decide to write a story, we face a myriad of questions with regard to plot, characters, genre, word choices, style, and much more. These are questions only we, the author, can answer.

The good news is that we have unlimited choices.

The bad news is—yup, you guessed it—we have unlimited choices.

Which makes our job interesting, but also extremely challenging. If we are indecisive, stop asserting ourselves and making the necessary choices—which can be as inconsequential as "What color will my heroine's hair be?" or as critical as "Should I kill off this character?"—we hit a wall of uncertainty. Fearing we're inadequate to the task of making these critical choices, and ever completing the book, we can't move forward. It's what we sometimes call "writer's block."

This feeling of being overwhelmed, and its accompanying fear of failure, can truly be crippling. We need to remind ourselves that there are very few truly bad choices for our story. Many are just marginally better than others. We just need to take our best shot, then go with it and see what happens. Nothing is written in stone. We can always change our minds later.

### *Always Write Forward*

When drafting a story, it's best to keep moving forward. Don't look back. That's one of our rules as Extreme Novelists.

Don't stop writing, even if the ground beneath your feet feels shaky. Even if you're convinced you're straddling the San Andreas Fault of the literary world and the seismograph is registering top of the Richter scale. Just type. I promise you this:

*The best way to break writer's block is by the physical act of doing the work.*

It is by writing freely, from the beginning of our earliest draft to its end, letting our subconscious do as much of the work as possible, that allows us to experiment and, eventually, to see the big picture. Along the way, we'll come up with alternate ideas for characters, action, dialogue. We can make use of these as we move forward. During the revision process, we can play with alternatives. But for now, we stay the course.

As long as you are willing to make choices, whether they are permanent or temporary, you will continue to move forward, steadily adding to our novel. And by writing daily, "living in the book," your voice (not to mention your craft) will grow stronger and stronger. With this strength comes confidence in your ability to write a compelling story.

### *Choosing to Compromise*

One of the many choices you will make while you're planning and executing your novel involves balancing your vision of the story with the needs of your readers. We first mentioned this in the last chapter.

In other words, even as you are writing your story, you will consider marketing issues. Because, after all, liking your own book is a given, but getting others to like your book doesn't just happen. Reader appeal is something the author can control, at least to a certain extent.

To start with, ask yourself *who* you are writing this story for. Who is your audience?

If you are spinning a tale purely for your own amusement and satisfaction, and you never expect another soul to read it, there's no need to consider the reading tastes of others. You can totally skip this section and move on to other issues. But if you wish to see your novel published and read by as many others as possible, you may want to take into account the age, sex, interests, education, or genre preferences of your hoped-for readers.

This doesn't mean selling your soul. It doesn't require giving up on your vision of the story or drastically altering your writing style. What it does mean is, sometimes, making subtle compromises.

When I begin working on a new novel, I'm always terribly excited about the process. Ideas flit through my head. Amazing possibilities tempt me. I'm enthralled with my new characters and eager to see how they will play out the drama of their lives. However,

# THE EXTREME NOVELIST

I know I can't completely ignore my readers' needs. After all, the practical side of me would really prefer to see some positive reviews to encourage sales. So before I begin writing, I consciously decide who it is that I'm writing for.

To be honest, most of the time I'm writing for adult women. And because I think that love, in all of its many glorious forms (parental, sibling, sexual, romantic, or religious) is a fascinating and important part of life, one or another form of love will play a significant role in my story.

I also get a kick out of tales of mystery, suspense, mayhem, dark secrets, and thrills. They're what I grew up reading. Arthur Conan Doyle's wonderfully evocative adventures featuring Sherlock Holmes swept me away to the foggy streets of Victorian London. I also adored Nancy Drew stories, science fiction written by Isaac Asimov, and the early-colonial adventures of Kenneth Roberts. So it's no wonder that I enjoy writing novels that feature suspense, mystery, a little romance, and hopefully a great adventure.

Decide what sort of story you'll write then determine your probable audience based on your goals. Do you plan to write scary monster tales to entertain boy readers, ages 10–15? Or do you hope to appeal to mature readers of both sexes by writing a whopper of an espionage-thriller?

One writer told me that, because of her previous experience in publishing action-adventure comic books for many years, she has acquired a modest following of male readers, who are now between sixty and seventy years old. They are a ready audience for her new novels, and she keeps their tastes in mind. She makes sure to include car chases, big weapons, and things that blow up.

If you know the genre within which you are going to write and have a sense of who your readers will most likely be, you'll have a lot better idea of how to focus your story in a way they will enjoy. Knowing your reader actually makes the job of writing easier. Some of your choices in theme, material, or level of sophistication will have been made for you. Even more importantly, if you're hoping to sell many copies of your book, you'll have a ready-made audience. And this will help immensely when you get around to launching your book and publicizing it.

It's tempting to try to follow trends. Maybe you've heard that vampire stories or erotica sell exceptionally well. (And they do!) But if that particular type of story doesn't top your list for personal reading, you'll be clueless as to the tricks and tropes that work for these types of fiction.

Fans of a particular brand of literature easily pick up on an author's lack of sincerity or paint-by-number writing. If they are disappointed or offended, they can be quite vocal in a blog review or on a website like Goodreads.com. We usually write our best if we choose to work within a genre that we enjoy reading, one with which we've become intimately familiar over time.

Do you adore reading Westerns complete with cowboys and gunfights? Or fantasies involving wizards and spells? Do bittersweet love stories that bring on tears warm your heart and brighten your day?

Whatever sort of story you gravitate toward when selecting the next book you'll read for pleasure—that's your best bet for writing. You've already absorbed many of the "rules" that govern the genre simply by reading good stories of that particular type.

Maybe you dream of penning the great American novel, a literary masterpiece that will be taught in college classrooms across the country. The next *To Kill a Mockingbird*. Go for it! But you may also want to consider writing a different kind of story someday. One that's less demanding on you as a writer and will draw a broad audience of popular-fiction readers. And therefore be more in demand by agents and publishers, and easier to place. Write a book for yourself—your dream book—and then a book for the rest of the world, for the fun of it. This is a compromise, but it's a generous and pleasant one.

### *Be a Savvy Prewriting Researcher*

If you wish to make writing fiction your next career, paying attention to what publishers are printing and readers are reading is critical. Spend time in bookstores. Chat with booksellers or librarians. Notice which novels seem to be selling well and are on wait lists at the library.

Focus on novels published within the past five years, not the classics we've all loved—or been forced to read in school. Today's publishing world is an entirely different animal than what existed twenty or more years ago. See if you can identify patterns of interest that coincide with your own reading and writing tastes.

Catching a trend that matches your enthusiasm is possible but usually only when it's relatively new. And then, only if you're a very fast writer. Readers' tastes are fickle. You might be able to get a manuscript or two written before the fad fades, or you may miss the boat entirely.

This is another good reason for writing a fast first draft. If we take five years or more to complete a novel, based on what we feel is working well for writers today (and the technology available to us), the literary world may well have moved on and morphed into something different by the time we have a full manuscript in hand.

But there is yet another reason for rapid writing (aside from its value in silencing The Voices.) Yes, readers' tastes change, but *we* change, too.

As people and as word crafters, we are forced to adapt to what life throws at us. We are constantly bombarded by events related to our health, our family, our job, even to world events. Within five, ten, or more years, we have changed in relationship to the world around us. Indeed, even our perception of the world and humankind may have taken a sharp turn.

Our writing, too, transforms, ever improving, becoming more sophisticated, subtler, hitting the mark with less effort. And so, parts of the book we started writing years ago, and we're now trying to finish, may feel quite alien to us. "Did I really write this?"

It's almost as if we are reading someone else's work. Another person on reading the novel that took you a decade to write may wonder if two different people had a hand in writing it. Which probably isn't very far from the truth.

By writing a fast and furious first draft, we stand the best chance of matching our original vision for the book. Because the world, *and all of us in it*, keep evolving.

### *Control vs. Mayhem*

One of the most important choices an author makes when writing fiction, which contributes to the voice of a particular book, has to do with the story's perspective or point-of-view scheme. We mentioned POV earlier with regard to bonding reader and character. Now let's think about this tricky element of fiction in more depth.

Understanding how best to control perspective in a story means the difference between a sharply focused, easy-to-follow plot and a story that doesn't live up to its full potential.

Several basic perspective plans are available to us when we write fiction. If you are already well-versed in these options, and feel confident in selecting and working with one of these, it's okay to skip ahead. But Point of View is such a critical element of the writing process that I encourage you to take this opportunity for a quick review.

We spend time in almost every class that I teach talking about viewpoint. It's one of the least understood and most underused tools available to novelists. Even experienced authors sometimes fail to grasp how to best take advantage of perspective. Admittedly, mastering the concept of perspective can be challenging. In fact, entire books have been written on this one facet of fiction writing. For now, though, let's just look at three basic plans from which we might choose for our story's POV.

They are:

> *Omniscient*
> *Single point of view*
> *Multiple, controlled point of view*

*Omniscient* perspective appeals to many new writers. Although I put it at the top of the list for the purpose of explanation, it is probably the least effective, the hardest to pull off effectively, and is considered by many editors today an old-fashioned style and therefore less useful for today's fiction.

An omniscient (meaning "all knowing") POV declares that we will be able to hear virtually any character's thoughts, at any time, and share with them their experiences and internal reactions. It provides the ultimate freedom to wander through characters' heads. It allows the author to take readers into any scene regardless of which characters happen to be there. In fact, none of the characters need to be shown in the scene. We can simply experience the action through an absent "narrator." It's as close as the reader can come to a God-like view of the world.

Ideally, the omniscient POV offers fluid movement through a variety of characters' interior monologues. We are given the greatest amount of insight into the minds of as many individuals as we like. Sounds great, doesn't it? The reader not only observes any action as it happens, he can be made aware of events that none of the characters know about.

But this siren's song of unlimited literary freedom is deceptive. It encourages authors to do what editors and agents refer to as "head hopping." And it's this rapid shifting at the author's whim from one character's thoughts to another's that wreaks havoc with the focus and flow of a story. Readers have to work harder to figure out whose head they're in. Tracking the main character becomes more difficult, and we feel less connected with the most important character.

So what alternatives are available to us?

The extreme opposite of omniscient is a *Single Point of View*. In that case we choose one character in the story and remain solely within that character's mind throughout the entire book. This means we need to develop a very interesting and appealing character with whom our readers will bond early in the story and wish to follow. The reader may even feel they are sharing a virtual reality with this character. The emotional connection can be very powerful. The downside is that you can only show what this character observes.

Still another choice is the *Controlled, Multiple Point of View*. In this case we have much more freedom than a single POV to move between the thoughts of a select few characters. But we don't jump around at random, in and out of our characters' heads. In fact we are clever enough to use either a chapter break or a shift between scenes to finish using the perspective of one character, and then open in another character's mind in a new scene or chapter. This plan enables the reader to follow several characters throughout the story without risking confusion or POV whiplash.

After all, our job as author isn't to prove how clever we are by building a novel that is so complex and convoluted the reader has to struggle to untangle the story's meaning. Rather, we should be gracious and allow our readers to feel *they* are smart because they are able to "get" the point of the novel.

The choice is ultimately yours, of course. Whether you select an omniscient point of view, a single point of view, or a multiple point of view depends upon how comfortable you are at handling that style of writing. It also depends upon the type of story you're telling. A traditional detective story might employ a single viewpoint, through the eyes and experiences of the sleuth who is the main character. But a historical novel or a family saga, with several almost equally important characters, might better be served by a controlled, multiple perspective.

We might choose two characters to tell our story. Or three or six. Maybe even more, if necessary. But remember what we said earlier about using only as many characters as we *need* in a story. The same is true for choosing your perspective plan. Fewer is usually better. The more characters' perspectives we investigate, the weaker the connection between reader and main character.

Lesson learned? Best to think ahead if you can. Look for ways to limit the perspective in your story *before you start writing*. If you're already well into your draft, come up with a new plan and begin using it now. When you start your revisions, you will alter the earlier-written scenes as necessary to reflect your more controlled and effective POV plan.

### *Untangle Those Dang Pronouns!*

Once you've determined your viewpoint arrangement, you'll want to decide how you'll refer to your POV character(s) and other characters. It's important that this choice be consistent throughout the novel.

Omniscient perspective demands the use of third-person narrative. That is, using he/she to refer to each character according to gender. Using "I" to describe every single character in the story would simply overwhelm and frustrate readers.

If you are using a single character's POV all the way through the novel, you can choose first-person ("I") or third-person ("he/she") narration. Either works well. Elect to use whichever you, the writer, feel most comfortable with and best suits the story. But take into consideration the type of tale you're telling. The intimacy that develops between a first-person character and reader is hard to beat, but its limitations may create problems for you down the road if you wish to show action this character can't observe.

Multiple point-of-view stories, traditionally, have used third person. However, in today's fiction authors often experiment with styles by alternating between first-person and third-person narration. Or even giving three or four characters their own story and allowing each one a turn at being "I." These are viable possibilities only if you are very careful to tip off readers so that they understand when you're shifting from one character's viewpoint to another's.

For instance, if you feel strongly about writing in first person, but you realize you'll need more than one perspective to tell your story, you may want to clue in the reader by labeling chapters according to the name of the character in whose head the reader will reside for the duration of that chapter. Or, if you wish to be more subtle, use dialogue, action, or descriptive clues at the very start of a scene so that the reader immediately understands we're no longer following Fred and have moved on to experiencing the action through William. (e.g., The next day William left the apartment before Fred woke up. He walked a mile to the park.) However you do it, keeping the reader's comfort in mind is the best way to avoid confusion and give your writing a strong structure. Do that and you're on your way to impressing the professionals, and maybe even harpooning a publishing contract.

### *Keep It Simple*

It never ceases to amaze me how often debut authors contrive to make the job of writing their first novel more difficult than it needs to be.

At the beginning of this book we acknowledged that writing a novel is a big deal. In many ways it's an extreme accomplishment. It's a project that requires an enormous gob of time, intense thought, and physical energy. It nearly always requires the sacrifice of other projects, absolute dedication on the author's part, and delicate fine tuning of the nearly finished novel.

When considering the basic genre and style in which you'd like to write, it makes sense (at least early in our careers) to make the job of writing as easy on ourselves as possible. Save the groundbreaking, experimental prose and novelty structures for a later book. Save for another time that clever structure you devised. You know, the one requiring seven characters' perspectives as each one recalls, in his own way and excruciating detail, the same incident!

If you want to get your first (or second or third) novel finished, and then published and read by as many people as possible, focus on the story and tell it in the most direct and interesting way. The classic formula of writing in the past tense with a single first- or third-person POV will work as well for you and your reader as it has for thousands of books before yours. Or select just two or three viewpoints and stick to them.

You don't need to break new ground to tell a great story. By making simpler, tried-and-true choices for your novel's set-up, you'll be able to concentrate on the story itself, creating vivid characters and scenes that will capture your reader's imagination and heart.

THE EXTREME NOVELIST

## Chapter 9: Pacing the Novel and Yourself

As we Extreme Novelists work our way through the rough draft of our novel—ninety minutes a day, six days a week—it pays to be aware of two kinds of pacing. One involves the story's plot. The other, our writing speed.

Most often when we speak about the pacing of a story, we're interested in holding the reader's attention. We want to make sure that every chapter, virtually every scene, moves the story another step closer to the novel's climax and resolution, without unnecessary lag time. The momentum of the action and intensity of the characters' emotional involvement should build toward the story's conclusion.

If, however, we indulge ourselves in the luxury of lapsing into lengthy descriptive passages unrelated to the story's action or the characters' personal struggles, the momentum drops off. And so does the reader's interest.

### *Avoid Wandering*

Why on earth would a writer do this? Go wandering off into unconnected material.

It's tempting to take our readers on a tour of our last vacation destination, the town where we grew up, or an exotic setting we've concocted in our own head. We may be compelled to use every scenic detail, thinking we're enriching our story. Writers with a legal background may feel the urge to show off their expertise by spending twenty pages in a courtroom scene that drags the story nearly to a halt. Historians have so many facts stored away in their brains, they find it hard to pull out just a few telling details and not indulge themselves in teaching the rest of us everything they know about the twelfth century.

Leisurely plotting, involved description, and word play may have been perfectly acceptable to readers decades ago. But writing styles have changed.

Students often say they wish to write like their favorite author—Hemingway, Fitzgerald, or Proust. But those authors, as we've already discussed, weren't competing with 3-D movies, special-effects videos, and gaming programs for their readers' attention. For those interested in writing popular fiction today—that is any of the genres except literary or experimental fiction—keeping our pacing taut, and ruthlessly cutting out clutter that slows the reader's heartbeat and reduces tension, are critical skills.

Ultimately, nothing should interfere with your story's flow.

Yes, beautiful words may stream from pen to paper, or fingertips to keyboard. More power to you if they do! But along with that lovely prose, don't forget to keep the action moving and vivid, enabling the reader to feel "present" in the story. Involved. There's real danger in falling so in love with our voluptuous phrases and clever imagery that we become blind to the fact we're wandering from the narrative.

Beautiful writing will certainly enhance any well-designed story. But story has to come first.

### *Sustain Your Personal Pace*

The other type of pacing has to do with the speed with which an author writes. If you are writing quickly, thereby allowing your subconscious to do more of the heavy lifting, you should be accumulating pages at a fairly rapid pace. If you've set your daily goal of writing ninety minutes (or more) each day, but the minutes seem to leak away unproductively as you screen stare or look up facts, then you might find it helpful to give yourself a page-number goal for the day instead of a time limit.

Can you normally expect to write three pages a day? Five? Eight? (Here, again, we're talking about imperfect writing. Just getting the bones of the story down.)

If you find yourself writing just one or two pages each day, you're probably making the job of writing a rough draft harder than it needs to be. Writing overly cautiously, weighing each word, this constrains creativity and silences the subconscious.

Several professional writers I know (myself included) set a daily limit of ten pages per day to keep ourselves honest. I know I need to keep my fingers moving on the keyboard and not daydream if I want to get out of my office that day.

Most importantly, reassure yourself that now isn't the time to worry about spelling, grammar, or complex setting details, all of which can be accuracy checked or added in later. That's called revising, and it's not part of our job description at the moment.

All we're doing for now is telling ourselves the story. Getting as much of this tale down on screen or paper in its natal form, even as we learn it. We're working on structure and the big picture. Detail work slows us down and must, of necessity, come later. Once we have the entire story blocked out, we can make the writing pretty, correct errors, elaborate with imagery and lush details, as long as it doesn't bury the story.

"But won't rushing the writing in this way make a terrible mess of my novel? If I never question or criticize myself, or I fail to search out the best words to express my meaning, aren't I condemning my literary brainchild to mediocrity, at best? I don't want to be a hack!"

You aren't and you won't be. This draft is never intended to be a finished product. It's by releasing the creative muse to do what it does best—spill out the story with as few restrictions as possible—that enables us to get all the way through a book in a reasonable amount of time.

How many times have you started to write a novel? How many times have you managed to write one, two, maybe three chapters then stalled out? This usually happens because we have chosen to shut down the creative part of our brain and start criticizing our work. We've told our brain, "What I've written here just isn't good enough. I need to stop and make it right. I need to make it perfect or no one will ever want to read the rest of the book."

Once you attempt to throw that switch in your brain (you remember, the one that doesn't exist), shutting down the artist-writer and turning on the ruthless critic, you've severely reduced your chances of writing to the end.

Give yourself permission to use your creative energy first, and exclusively, all the way through the manuscript to the very last sentence. Don't criticize. Don't correct yourself. And don't look back!

When you have drafted the full story—beginning, middle, and end—that's the right time to pat yourself on the back, break out the Champagne, take a few days' break. Then, and only then, change hats and become the critic and editor. Then you can dig out errors, revise, polish, and wordsmith in minute detail. But for now, concentrate on moving forward on your beautifully creative and messy draft. That's your sole responsibility for now.

### Leave Notes

"But what if I need to make major changes to my plot or characters, and I'm already a third of the way through the draft? What if the synopsis I wrote when I started out no longer applies?"

Not a problem.

One of the reasons we allow the synopsis to remain fluid is to enable improvements along the way. You don't need to stop and rewrite a synopsis whenever you come up with a new idea. And, as we've already stated, you don't need to revisit earlier chapters and rewrite them. It's far less risky to simply add a note reminding yourself of the change you wish to make—then continue writing forward as if that new idea is already part of the story.

Keep track of changes and new ideas as they occur to you. Note them directly in the digital file of the manuscript, in handwritten notes on a printed copy of the manuscript, or in a writing log.

By leaving a quick note-to-self, either within the problematic chapter (I type messages to myself in capital letters, then highlight them in yellow) or the synopsis, you avoid interrupting the exciting forward flow of your imagination. You are creating a list of assignments for yourself, which later will become part of the revision process.

You may write something like: *Remember to add Jennifer to this scene. She needs to be introduced before the murder.* Or: *Add hero's motivation here.* Or: *Change setting from the grocery store to heroine's kitchen.*

By freeing yourself of revision jobs that should come later, you won't constantly retrace your steps or fret over elements of the story that are best dealt with more thoughtfully later. You'll make much faster progress on your draft and avoid second-guessing yourself.

Enjoy the speed and creative surge you'll get from seeing your pages pile up. Write daily. Write forward. Ignore the voices that predict disaster. They are powerless over an Extreme Novelist.

### *Keep it Lean*

New authors often ask how long scenes, chapters, or an entire novel should be. There is no standard length for any of these. However, most literary agents today suggest limiting the overall word count for a first novel to eighty thousand or fewer words.

Production costs discourage acquiring editors from buying lengthier novels if written by authors without a track record for substantial sales. In general, today's fiction tends to be leaner than even a dozen years ago, with shorter scenes, chapters, and sentences.

*Why is this?*

Readers have become so accustomed to Hollywood's habit of flashing in and out of scenes on TV and movie screens that they get impatient with lengthy episodes in novels. By breaking up the narrative into smaller chunks—chapters themselves and scenes within chapters—the writer can give the reader a sensation of rapid-fire pacing.

Shorter, but still complete, scenes and chapters also give the author more opportunities for suspenseful end-of-scene moments. These minicliffhangers work well for modern readers, holding their attention and urging them forward with increased tension. Since every scene has a beginning, middle, and end—just like every chapter and every book—we can also view these shorter episodes as distinct little bites to make our writing job easier.

If you're feeling overwhelmed by the thought of writing an entire book, say to yourself, "Today all I'm doing is writing just one five-page scene. Anyone can do that!" By frequently reminding ourselves of the day's limited writing task, we remove the pressure we often put upon ourselves.

Don't think: *OMG! I'm writing a freaking book. This is so hard!*

Think: *I'm just telling my reader about this one incident in my character's life. Easy-peasy.*

If your scenes average about five pages each, and you write at least one scene each day, six days a week, you'll have forty-eight scenes at the end of eight weeks. And guess what? That gives you

240 pages. In standard format (12 pt font/double-spaced lines), you can figure you have around sixty thousand words. Which is more than enough as a first draft for a novel.

Your page count will vary according to how closely you stick to your daily writing program, and how many pages you can draft each day. The important thing to remember is that this is doable. Set your goal, keep up your pace (and the story's), and you'll have a rough draft of a novel in eight or so weeks.

### *Use Extreme Novelist's Methods to Get the Job Done*

Writers often compare writing tools or methods with one another, but we tend to limit these discussions to the most obvious.

Do you write on a computer or with a pen on a legal pad?

Do you work at a desk in your office or curled up in an easy chair at home?

Do you use a writing program like Scrivener, prefer to organize your notes on index cards, or keep the details in your head?

The question of how we actually write is a relevant one. But given that many novelists struggle with finding time to write at all, an even more critical question is: How do we fit writing into our everyday routine and make it part of our busy life?

#### High-energy Times

Earlier in this book we discussed the idea of recognizing and protecting our most productive times of the day or night. Have you been able to pinpoint yours? Have you targeted at least ninety minutes, six days a week in which to do nothing but write? If not in one chunk (say, first thing in the morning), then in pockets of time that will add up to at least an hour and a half of dedicated writing time?

If you've tried a couple of possibilities and none has worked out yet, keep experimenting with options. Be creative. What suits one person may be impossible or just plain uncomfortable to another.

During different phases in my writing life, the hours in which I've been able to write have altered drastically. When my children were very young I was sometimes able to protect and use thirty or more minutes during their nap times to write, then rely on another hour after they were in bed. Parents frequently can use a nap themselves when the little ones are asleep, but if we're focused on getting our book written, those golden minutes of silence are ripe to be seized and turned into a short scene.

However, children eventually outgrow naps and early bedtimes. Then what?

### The Sound Cave

Once my kids had outgrown naps, but could entertain themselves for an hour at a time with minimum supervision, I could type while they played. If their games happened to be particularly exuberant and disruptive to my thoughts, I created a sound cave for myself by using noise-reduction earphones and playing music over the clamor of their recreation. You still can hear distress sounds that signal an emergency. If a child is hurt or frightened, you'll know it. The earphones just muffle noise enough to let it fade into the background.

Directly outside the window in my current home-office is my neighbor's backyard. She runs a home daycare service. Unless it's raining or snowing, half a dozen exuberant children play in her yard on most days. It would be useless for me to step outside and plead with the little darlings, "Keep it down, please. Writer at work." And so I simply clamp on my earphones and fall into one of my favorite violin concertos.

### Sound Tracks

Are you in the habit of sharpening a handful of pencils, reorganizing your desk, or cleaning out a closet before you can start writing? Replace a time-killing warm-up routine with a personalized sound track.

Many authors I know have discovered the advantages of creating a unique sound track for each novel they work on. When you play favorite or specially selected music over and over again, it becomes a background score to your story's plot, characters, and setting.

This is very similar to the mood music that heightens the experience of a motion picture. Two CDs, or their equivalent in length from a collection of individual tracks, will provide you with the appropriate amount of writing time. Each time you sit down to write, slip on your earphones and key up your sound track.

After working to this particular music two or three times, you'll find your brain begins to connect the story with the recording. This is an excellent way to immerse yourself in your daily writing. Whenever you repeat the routine of putting on the earphones, turning on the music, resting fingers on keyboard—you will feel instantly transported into your story's world. There's little or no transition time.

No longer are minutes wasted while you try to remember where you left off. Initial screen staring is reduced or eliminated. You're productive and enjoying your favorite music, so you're more relaxed as well.

Stephen King, I'm told, writes to classic rock. One romance author told me that she always writes to Top Forty songs. I avoid any music that has lyrics. I start hearing the words in the song instead of the words in my head that should be part of the book. So I work exclusively to instrumental music. My preference is for classical violin. I find the passion and tone of the violin energizing but also calming.

Pick whatever type of music you find most enjoyable and conducive to writing. If you're working on historical fiction you might even choose music composed during that era, if you can find it. The key is to submerge yourself in your story by whatever means necessary, as quickly as possible.

### Mobile Writing

The opposite of creating a sound cave is training yourself to be immune to outside sounds and thus become a mobile writer. When you learn to write outside of the confines of your usual work area (kitchen, office, the library), you create virtual writing dens where you will be comfortable and learn to tune out the clatter and distractions of your surroundings.

The location can be as noisy and busy as any you can imagine and still be a great place for writing. Just the idea of writing under such conditions horrifies many writers, but moving outside of your habitual place of work can be incredibly freeing. We witnessed an example of this when we discussed my student's dilemma; his roommates made it impossible to write in the apartment the four young men shared.

Once you have trained yourself to write publicly, you can take yourself off to a coffee shop, shopping mall, park, or virtually anywhere—and function in an invigorating atmosphere. It actually helps that you're not feeling isolated from the rest of humanity. Unlike the use of noise-blocking earphones, this technique depends upon the anonymity of public spaces.

When you write in a restaurant or a similar location, no one is there to demand your attention or ask anything of you. (Other than: "Would you like a refill of that coffee?") No one will come up to you and ask you to stop writing and make them a sandwich, help with homework, clean up the kitchen, or even just talk to you. You won't be tempted to throw an extra load of clothes into the washing machine, wash the car, or take the dog for a walk. You've put chores and responsibilities, other than your writing, at a comfortably remote distance.

And what about the noise of conversations and people moving through public places? Unless you're unfortunately seated next to a screaming infant, the sounds around you become a wash of white sound as soon as you're engrossed in your story.

If you find yourself in a place that's so obscenely noisy you can't ignore the cacophony, then you simply whip out your earphones and boot up your sound track. Instant sound cave!

## Page Celebrations

Celebrating small accomplishments along the way is another great boost to any writing endeavor. I like to keep in my printer a stack of discarded paper, rescued from my husband's workplace. I print out scenes and chapters as I write, making use of the blank sides of the pages I'm recycling by putting them to a second use.

When my pages start to accumulate nicely, I visit my favorite office-supply store and buy a jazzy three-ring notebook to house a physical copy of my book. The binder I purchased for *The Extreme Novelist* draft was red "leather" (vinyl, but it does look real) with a big clear window on the front. I periodically experiment with my "cover art" by trying out digitally clipped images, magazine pictures, or photographs.

Seeing this notebook grow fatter and fatter day by day gives me a satisfying feeling. The work-in-progress begins to seem less imagined, more substantial. A real book!

An additional advantage to keeping a physical copy of my draft, aside from having another form of backup should my computer crash, has to do with revision. Later, when my first draft is complete, I'll need a printed copy to read and review. I find that reading only on a screen isn't enough. By reviewing in both formats, I catch different sorts of errors and come up with better ways to organize and fine-tune my novel.

A third reason for making a paper copy, I've just hinted at—I simply don't trust technology. I've witnessed too many disasters involving other people's crashed or stolen computers that contain most of a writer's creative life. So, of course, I back up my work.

At least every second day, I copy onto a flash drive. I also e-mail copies to myself and subscribe to a cloud service. But I can't break the rather obsessive old habit of keeping a hard copy of the book in my car's trunk "just in case."

After all, what are the chances of the house (and with it, my computer) burning to ashes AND the car being stolen on the same day? (I know. It's admittedly overkill. But protecting one's creative product is important.)

However, the very best thing about printing pages as you go is this: You get to wrap your creation in a colorful, important-looking binding and place it on the kitchen table to admire as you pass by a dozen times each day. Or you can carry it lovingly about with you wherever you go. Seeing the pages accumulate within the covers will encourage you to write forward, rather than be tempted to look back and rejigger what you've already done. (Remember, that comes later. Much later.)

What it comes down to is this. We have to find the best ways to write our books without letting the world impact us and, eventually, stop us from doing what our hearts tell us we must do.

Writers write. It's in our blood. When we are prevented from doing so, we're miserable, frustrated people. If you are meant to be a writer, you know whereof I speak.

THE EXTREME NOVELIST

**Negotiate Writing Time**

Sometimes we need to educate the people in our lives when it comes to protecting our writing time. To be fair, it's nearly impossible for someone who isn't a writer to understand the importance of our craft to us.

I know I warned of possible complications if we divulge our writing ambitions. But there comes a time when it's to our benefit to inform friends and loved ones of our needs as writers. If there's a lack of understanding, sometimes we can negotiate creative time and smooth the path to a more satisfying and effective writing schedule. And, as a bonus, we won't feel guilty about withdrawing into our virtual writer's cave.

One of my students, a young mother of two with a full-time job, became increasingly concerned about her husband's objections to her spending time working on her novel. He finally told Claire she would need to quit the course and stop writing because, he claimed, she was robbing her children, and him, of her attention.

Claire was close to tears as she told me this. Before the end of class that day, (which was to be the last class before she dropped out), we had a discussion about personal time. I asked if her husband might be willing to sit down and compare each of their "free" times during the week. She thought he'd be open to this. Later, she told me how this went.

They sat down one night with an assignment. Each was to write down on a piece of paper all of the minutes and hours out of each day, during a normal week, when they weren't either at their day jobs, the one responsible for the children, sleeping, or doing household chores. Then they compared their totals.

It turned out that Claire's husband had regular times during the week for activities he enjoyed: Thursday nights was poker night with the boys, two other days each week he worked out at the gym, and then there was the occasional hunting trip. Claire, on the other hand, could count her weekly free time in minutes. Her personal time was, for all purposes, nonexistent.

Her husband's response to this realization? "Well, huh, that doesn't seem fair." Smart guy!

He finally got it. They came to an agreement that she should have protected personal time, just as he had. If she wanted to use it for writing, that was her choice. They made a few adjustments in the family's schedule. Her husband agreed to take charge of the children for baths and bedtime stories two evenings each week so that she could write. She returned to the class as well. And they hired a babysitter for two hours on Saturdays.

Opportunities to negotiate your writing time present themselves in many forms. For many writers, time spent traveling—whether it's for vacation, work, or visiting relatives—becomes a challenge. We feel as though we can't write because extra social or business demands are placed upon us, and then there's the general disruption of travel. Our writing falls by the wayside.

But this needn't happen.

Recently my husband decided to fly from DC to the Texas coast to visit his sister. He wanted me to accompany him. We would be staying at his sister's house. The trip would give him a break from his intense work schedule, enable him to reunite with old friends from high school days, and provide me with interesting settings for future stories. All good!

Except for one thing. I was on book deadline.

According to my calculations, I needed to continue writing at least ten pages per day to have a manuscript ready to deliver to my editor and meet my contractual obligations. My being late would cramp her editing time and might delay the book's publication.

From previous experiences with family visits, I knew that sneaking in any serious writing time between socializing and group activities was going to be difficult. All the more so because people who don't write sometimes can't understand that we aren't being snooty or antisocial or selfish.

We're not isolating ourselves from others on a whim or out of rudeness. We're working because it's something we *must* do. It's a job like any other. For travelers it's even more crucial to "stay in the book" when we're in the middle of a project. If we don't write for a week or two, getting back into the story will be pure misery.

In cases like this, the writer needs to educate the nonwriters. We have no choice but to be proactive, drawing up ground rules in order to protect our creative time while avoiding misunderstandings and hurt feelings.

And so I told my husband if he wanted me along for the trip, I needed to have two uninterrupted hours each day in which to work.

"Fine. No problem," he said. "Just do what you need to do."

"No," I told him, "I need your help to make this work. You are going to call your sister before we go. Explain to her that I will be getting up early in the morning to write for two hours. This isn't a choice. It's necessary if I'm to come along. I will write from six to eight every morning. The rest of the day I'll be free for whatever the family decides to do. If I'm to come, she needs to be okay with this and inform the rest of the family."

He agreed that this seemed more than fair. I was asking him to help me protect a small percentage of each day we'd be visiting.

The first full day we were to spend at the family home, I got out of bed as planned, threw on a sweatshirt and jeans, and set up my laptop on the kitchen table. The rest of the family was still asleep. I held my breath, wondering whether this compromise would work. My sister- and brother-in-law weren't used to having a "writer-in-residence" and had a full slate of activities planned for the week. But I focused on my laptop screen, opened the manuscript file, and soon was pleasantly lost in my story.

The house remained silent for the next hour and, fresh from a good night's sleep, I got a lot done. Sometime during the second hour, I became vaguely aware of people beginning to stir in other rooms, but I was deep into my characters' lives by then. The hushed sounds barely penetrated my brain. I continued writing.

Toward the end of the two hours as I typed away, finishing a particularly exciting scene in my historical thriller (wherein I blew up a bridge over the Thames River), I heard the pitter-patter of feet entering the kitchen and the sound of a coffeepot beginning to gurgle as it perked away. But no one spoke to me, and so I remained "in the book" and working for another ten minutes.

At 8:00 a.m., my internal alarm went off. I had used up my allotted time, but that was fine. I felt mentally spent, and my page quota had been met. I knew if I continued trying to write my brain would have to work harder and my spine would stiffen up painfully. I saved and backed up my files then shut down for the day. Success!

Each subsequent day worked just as well. The key was preparation and education. Letting those around us know what we need from them, and listening to their needs in return, is always a good thing. But as writers we sometimes have to go the extra mile by demonstrating for our family and friends the ways in which a writer works. Only then can we avoid frustration on our part and theirs.

### Naysayers

Then again, there is no guarantee that a plea for writing time will be honored. There are always a few people who will persist in undervaluing what we are trying to do. It happens to both male and female writers of any age. A spouse, partner, child, neighbor, or workmate seems unable or unwilling to understand why our craft is so important to us.

You and I know that writing a novel is an amazing adventure. It's exercise for the mind, as well as the pursuit of a cherished and proud literary tradition. People who can't create as we do, or choose not to try because they fear failure, may discourage us from our writing goals. They may not intend to be cruel, but sometimes they are.

Before I published my first novel, I taught at a private school. Many of the other teachers knew I was writing stories, trying to get published, and seemed supportive. But as soon as I announced that I was leaving teaching and taking a less demanding (and lower-paying) job elsewhere to buy more time to complete my novel, they became very "concerned" for me. Not one of them looked pleased on hearing my announcement. They told me in various ways that they doubted the wisdom of what I was doing. They warned me that the chances of ever becoming published were incredibly small. I was giving up my teaching career and a decent income on a long shot that was destined for failure.

I prefer to believe that each of them was sincere in suggesting that I not set my heart on publication, and were only trying to protect me. But I knew I had to at least try. After all, we make our own opportunities. Right?

Years later, I returned to that same school to address a student assembly as a published author. Many of those same naysayers came up to me and congratulated me—admitting they were truly amazed at my accomplishment. But I explained to them that what I'd done wasn't terribly special. I'm not a genius. I'm not particularly gifted. I simply practiced my craft until I earned my ten thousand hours and mastered the challenges all fiction writers face.

I honestly believe that anyone who truly wants to write and publish their stories can do it. But they must be willing to put in substantial and honest time and consistent effort.

If you work quickly through your rough drafts, concentrating on learning the story and discovering your characters through the scenes into which you place them, this explosion of storytelling rubs off on the tempo of the novel. So that even after you've done multiple revisions and fleshed out scenes that were thin, that wonderful, raw enthusiasm from your first draft will remain in the writing. This active, emotional, compelling fiction is almost impossible for readers to put down.

## Chapter 10: The Muddle In the Middle

If you've been writing your novel as you read this book, each day adding to your written pages, you may well have reached the middle of your book by now. Congratulations!

For the purpose of this course, let's say the middle of a novel begins somewhere after the second or third chapter and continues until we reach the long-awaited climax and resolution of the story. For the initial chapters of a book, we typically glide along on our enthusiasm for the great concept we've come up with. We're in love with our story!

Sometimes the process can feel almost effortless. *Wow! I'm on the express lane! Just zooming along and enjoying the ride*. It's easy to ignore our usual self-doubts. The negative chatter in our head, or from other people, seems distant. Ah, the writing life—marvelous!

Then one day we're working on chapter 4 (or 8 or 20) and we're suddenly blindsided by an attack of mind-numbing terror. We fear that:

1) We've run out of things to say. Or,

2) The end of the story is just around the corner, but the book is way too short. (Like thirty thousand words too short!) Or,

3) We have no idea how to get from where we are in the plot to any sort of logical resolution!

"What am I supposed to do now?" you moan. You glare at the ceiling and think what a waste of time this book-writing delusion has been.

Well, you're not alone. Somewhere in the middle of just about every novel written is an author throwing up his hands in frustration. He may trudge painfully onward, adding more pages to his book, but he no longer thinks of it as his masterpiece. The honeymoon is over. This adventure has turned into deadly hard work. It isn't at all what he had hoped for when he dreamed of becoming a novelist.

When the satisfaction and joy of writing evaporates into the air, we fear we'll never recapture that precious euphoria we once felt. Now writing has become just another dreaded task to add to the day's to-do list. Sadly, it's the easiest job to drop, because no one is threatening to fire you if you don't keep writing.

The reason inspiration and energy desert us is because we have used up our initial store of ideas. If we force ourselves to simply push on, feeling bored and uninspired, dragging ourselves through dull, repetitive scenes that seem to go nowhere, the reader will sense your ennui, and likewise become bored. And put down the book. That is, if we ever actually finished writing it.

We've all read novels in which we sensed the author was treading water. The plot fails to move forward, may actually feel as if it's replaying itself. The rushing river of exciting scenes has dwindled to a barely trickling stream.

But ideas, and with them inspiration, can be renewed. So here's what we need to do.

First, we know that the standard novel for adult readers, when finished, needs to be at least a minimum length—say around sixty thousand words—to be considered a book. (As we discussed earlier, a final draft of a debut novel can be up to eighty thousand words, or a little more, and still get a fair read from a literary agent or acquiring editor of a traditional publishing firm.) So we will concentrate on shaping the first draft to a length that—either through fleshing out details or cutting clutter—will approach this safest length: 60–80,000 words.

Strong middles are what saves novels from inducing yawning attacks in both the author and the reader. In fact, smack dab in the center of a book is where many, many jobs need to be done that can't be accomplished earlier in the story. It's *not knowing* what to do that leaves us feeling confused, as if we've lost our way in the midst of our own fantasy.

Once we add up all of the opportunities and tools available to us that will enhance the story and speed the book forward to completion, we will recover our original enthusiasm for the story. When middles are deftly handled, the tale becomes more complex, layered, even more appealing.     Let's check out some of these options for central chapters of any novel.

### *Deepen Characterization or Add a New Character*

Let's review some of what we've learned; it will only take a moment.

One of the errors we try to avoid at the outset of a novel is overwhelming the reader with assorted data. We called this an "information dump." Literary agents have also been known to refer to this as "throat clearing." Even if we writers think the information is important, and we believe in our hearts that we really should let the reader in on these critical facts and details, we must restrain ourselves.

The fact is, readers just want a good story. And they want it *now*! Not starting in chapter 2 or on page 40. That's why we provide a hook and a rapid start for our story with an early introduction of the central conflict.

Our audience may also be willing to be enlightened or to learn painlessly. But one thing readers definitely don't want is to be forced to meet one after another member of your cast—as if they've been dragged into a stranger's family reunion.

Readers keep turning pages and continue to enjoy the middle parts of a novel for the chance to learn more about the people. Keeping some information back about your most important characters, and then letting the reader gradually discover their habits, likes and dislikes, dreams, secrets, and fears is a smart strategy. You'll hoard surprises, until just the right time—most likely somewhere in the middle of the book. And, in fiction, surprises are good!

Oftentimes, physical descriptions can also wait until an appropriate moment in the story, when your POV character is able to observe him/herself or another person. If that natural opportunity comes early in the story, that's fine. If not, hold off until a bit later in the book.

When the reader gets a chance to view one character through the eyes of another, we stay inside the story. It's a very effective technique that avoids the need for the author to speak directly to the reader. Once the reader loses that dreamlike experience of being lost in a story, she may need time to recover before feeling fully engaged again.

In addition, it would seem more logical for a character to have the time and presence of mind to note details when a scene's action isn't too intense. (e.g., If I were running for my life, it's highly unlikely I'd be thinking about the color of my attacker's eyes or the pretty rose bush I just raced past.)

In general, we're better off steering clear of a laundry list of character traits. Do I, as a reader, care if the hero is exactly six foot two, wears size-eleven shoes, has two-inch sideburns, and favors a green waistcoat over any other color? If these or other details are critical to the story, or reveal something important about the character, they can be introduced gradually through the middle of the book and as needed.

Indeed, some individuals may more naturally appear for the very first time well into the novel. Although, it's a good idea for a character to appear, or at least be mentioned by others, before they play a critical role in the story. Otherwise, their sudden arrival may seem contrived. They've popped up out of nowhere at the author's convenience.

### Do the Unexpected

This ability to gradually accumulate a cast of characters presents another opportunity for doing something fresh and unpredictable in middle chapters. Readers don't know that you're going to sneak another character or two into the story until it happens. The appearance of new faces and personalities refreshes the story and gives readers something unexpected and interesting to contemplate.

Who are these newcomers? Are they going to be helpful to the character we really care about or harm him? How might they impact the outcome of the story? Is one of these unknowns to blame for the murder? A valuable key to the mystery? A returning lover?

Consider which of your characters, if any, might stand in the wings until a middle chapter and surprise (shock?) the reader. Their striding on stage mid-drama just might feel more natural since, in real life, we are constantly adding or losing people from our circle of friends and family.

The late appearance also is a great way to prepare readers for a threatening character and to build tension. If, through the dialogue and thoughts of other characters in the story, readers learn how evil and vicious a particular person can be, we will instantly be on alert when we see him appear in the flesh. Tension automatically jumps sky high!

### *Bring in the Backstory*

We've learned ways to single out and choose an "instigating moment," that is, an incident that kicks off the action and sets the story rolling swiftly and inexorably toward resolution. Backstory is anything that happened before that moment in time. Although backstory can be the kiss of death if placed at the opening of a novel, it will fit nicely in the middle of your story.

The reason why many authors succumb to including prefaces, introductory notes, prologues, or instructional statements at the beginnings of their novels is, simply, *fear*. We are terrified of jumping straight into the plot without letting the reader know what we know. Our writer's brain warns us: "I'm the one who dreamed up this universe, this situation, these people. If I don't share with you everything I know, you won't understand what's going on."

*Beware, this is a trap!*

Readers are curious by nature. They *like* a good mystery. They *like* unraveling clues and analyzing details to come up with their own conclusions.

Forget about warming up your readers. Just launch straight into your story. Provide an appealing character your readers can care deeply about, who has a conflict that needs resolving. As you move through the story, you'll drop in more and more information gradually. Your audience will feel compelled to continue reading, learning as they go, until satisfied that they know everything they can know about the character they've bonded with, and he has safely arrived at the end of his adventure.

I realize it's possible to give examples of recent, award-winning novels that were slow going at the beginning because of the many, many pages devoted to backstory. These are today's rare rule breakers that rose above a weak opening. In fact, literary fiction depends less on plot and, when it has one at all, often wanders at a much more leisurely pace.

But in commercial fiction we aren't looking for the "hard-to-get-into" reaction from readers. That would be stacking the deck against ourselves.

If you simply can't make yourself wait to get this material out of your system before you begin writing the *real* chapter 1, then go ahead and write it. But after you've satisfied that urge to record your backstory, *remove it to a separate file and mark it for possible use in the middle of the novel.* That way, you won't feel you've wasted your time. When you reach appropriate middle chapters and need additional interesting material to continue developing your characters, you'll go to this file and select a bit of this information to flesh out your people and add weight to the story.

Whatever the reader needs to know about the people, places, history, or ideas presented in your story, you will have ample opportunity to divulge throughout the body of your novel. This is where you'll need fresh ammunition to hold readers' interest. This is where you can sprinkle new ideas, data, clues, flourishes, and yummy tidbits to entice the reader deeper and more intimately into your story-world.

### *Enrich Your Description Judiciously*

You may have saved comprehensive descriptions of characters and settings until you got your story rolling. If you have—congratulations! But once you've hooked readers and they are under the spell of the bond you've nurtured between them and the most important personalities in your story, you're free to play with additional setting, character, and technical details.

It's true, we don't want to bore or overwhelm readers with jargon or language so technical it's annoyingly incomprehensible. But if we always use the most common or generic term to describe a person, place, or thing—the writing begins to sound flat and unimaginative. Therefore we need to find a comfortable balance between straightforward wording (for the sake of clarity) and a rich vocabulary (to add interest).

Some readers today are offended by writers who use unfamiliar or "big" words, even though it's easy enough to Google these. You may take this into consideration, or not. I try to avoid showing off by leaning toward simple words that do the job. But if a longer or less familiar word is really the *right* word to get across my meaning—or I want to create a special effect, emotion, or mood—I use it.

When we select specific (not necessarily "fancy") wording over generic terms, we create a reality readers can immerse themselves in and believe in. Remembering that readers love to learn painlessly by reading fiction, we choose from among the vast array of details and descriptors that suit the job.

Shall we just call a tree a tree? Or will it be a willow, an ancient oak, or a sapling? Each specific word creates a very different visual image in the reader's mind. Does the queen's lady-in-waiting wear a dress? Or is it a gown, a frock, a chemise, a robe, or a polonaise? Is the heroine's house on a street somewhere in France? Or does she live on Boulevard Saint-Germain in the sixth arrondissement?

Precise words that create a crystal-clear image in the reader's mind add realism to any story. Even if the words are totally invented by the author, as is often the case in science fiction and fantasy. Using real cities, landmarks, restaurants, or other businesses brings readers into virtual scenes that otherwise might feel vague. If the reader has actually visited the place you name, its appearance in the story will create a special familiarity that readers love. "Hey, I've been there! I remember that cute little café."

Here too, in the middle of the book, is the perfect place to include traits and actions for characters that you've already introduced. If understanding a character's appearance and motivation is critical to understanding the story, readers sometimes need an occasional reminder. A heroine who is six foot three may need to stoop when walking through some doorways. In an alien environment, the sky may glow crimson at night, orange in the daylight, and appear azure blue only on stormy days. By refreshing our readers' minds, we are encouraging them to keep on believing in the story.

### *Plant a Clue or Hint*

Story middles are also a great place to slip in vital information that will either help to resolve the conflict or stand in the main character's way of success. This is particularly true in any sort of mystery novel. The detective, private eye, or amateur sleuth uncovers new knowledge that needs to be passed along to the reader and possibly other characters. These clues eventually add up to either discovering the identity of the bad guy or explaining how/why the evil has been perpetrated.

Characters in any kind of novel may discover new information that readers already know. In other words, the author has allowed the reader to observe or eavesdrop on scenes revealing information that one or more characters isn't aware of. This is a powerful method of building suspense and tension within a story. You might drop hints to the reader of oncoming danger. Because we worry about the character(s) we care about, we feel mounting tension, uncertainty, perhaps real fear. We wish we could warn those in peril but can only hold our breath and read on, hoping for the best.

It should be mentioned that, depending upon the genre, some readers will have more tolerance than others for details and description. In general, readers of historical fiction seek far more information about mannerisms and social customs, costumes, history, architecture, and furnishings.

Readers of thrillers and other heart-thumping adventure stories only want enough detail to create a vivid movie in their heads as they track the breathtaking pace of the story. Stop the action during a chase scene to describe the wallpaper in a room or name the flowers blooming in a garden? Best not. Thriller and suspense readers, more than any other kind, constantly demand to know, "What happens next? What happens next? OMG, what happens *now?*" For them pacing is everything.

### *Add More Stumbling Blocks*

Plots often sag in the middle of a novel because the protagonist has run out of excuses for not achieving the yearned for goal. It then becomes increasingly illogical that these characters can't resolve their issues. The conflict has become repetitive, boring, or on the verge of disappearing entirely. It's simply too easy to deal with. For the reader, if not for the characters, the story is over.

What's an author to do?

This is often the case in stories where the conflict relies almost solely on the characters' failure to communicate. ("If these two lovers would just *talk* about what's bothering them!") This is a particularly egregious error as far as editors are concerned. But readers are equally savvy and will wonder what the heck is *wrong* with these people. Can't they see that a simple conversation will make the problem go away?

The solution is to add more, slightly different, and increasingly insurmountable stumbling blocks through the middle of the novel. If a protagonist is too close to a solution of the central problem, make her job more difficult. Put her through hell! Seriously. Readers love drama, tension, suspense, and surprises. (*Will Sarah ever get herself out of this mess?*)

When I reach the middle of my novel's first draft and feel the story beginning to drag, I make a point of retiring to a comfy chair in the living room with legal pad, pen, and cup of tea. (Or red wine. Red wine is always an option for me!) I put my feet up, lean back, take a sip, and close my eyes for a few moments. Then I focus on the blank pad, just as when I brainstormed my synopsis.

This time, I write down as many new opportunities as come to me for making my hero's or heroine's life miserable. (Possibly my antagonist's as well.) I jot down a list of words or phrases that describe all manner of mayhem, without criticizing myself or analyzing relevance, motive, logic, or proper spelling. I use free association as much as possible, letting my subconscious do most of the work.

The idea is to make it as tough as possible for the central character to straighten out her life and achieve whatever goals she set for herself early in the story. Only when we're ready to wrap up the book—meaning it's long enough and suits us—will we allow the story to end. By writing down anything at all that comes to mind, we can capture possibilities for delaying the story's resolution and make the most of dramatic potential.

In *The Gentleman Poet*, heroine Elizabeth finds herself in dire straits. She has no family and her only means of staying off the cruel London streets is to agree to being a servant. When her mistress decides to sail to the New World, Elizabeth is forced to go with her. The poor girl has no control over her own life; her survival depends entirely upon others' goodwill. And there's very little of that in her world.

However, when she is marooned on an island along with other passengers of the wrecked ship, she faces the same challenges as everyone else. Now everyone is on equal footing. There is no food, no fresh water since nearly all of their supplies have been ruined by saltwater. Perhaps they'll find a way of using rainwater, but rescue is unlikely since mariners give wide berth to the island's hull-ripping coral shoals. Without shelter, the party is at the mercy of the elements. Neither Elizabeth nor her companions can hope to survive for very long. Or so it would seem.

It is ironic that these challenges to survival create for Elizabeth an opportunity to shine and build a new life for herself as a gifted cook. A life that will give her the respect of others and hope for the future. The middle chapters of this novel provide rich ground for this young woman to discover talents that will help her build a place for herself in the world, if they can ever get off the island. Readers still won't know if the ending will be a happy one, and that's good. It builds tension and drives them to keep turning pages, hoping for the best for Elizabeth.

Write down everything that could possibly make life incredibly nasty and hopeless for your characters. You can do this individually for your protagonist, your antagonist, and even for some of your supporting characters. Make a list of a dozen, twenty, fifty impediments to success, no matter how wild or unlikely they may at first sound.

Will the weather or another act of nature make the hero's journey almost impossible? What might one character knowingly, or innocently, do that will interfere with another character's happiness or achievement? Is there a "plan" the characters have cooked up that can go awry? Does a tragedy occur as we near the end of the story that will all but force your hero to give up?

Allowing your subconscious (your muse, if you will) to provide new and interesting plot ingredients for the middle of a story is a painless and entertaining way to continue growing a book. Put your list away for a day or two, let it brew a bit. When you take it out again for another look, you'll be astonished that some of these possibilities stand out as promising.

Simply eliminate those ideas that are totally outlandish and not useful. Combine two or three ideas that complement each other, and highlight those that stand alone and excite you the most. Use this brainstorming technique, and you'll never again run out of juicy material for the middle of your stories.

### Upping the Stakes

In life, we often need to pay a price to get what we want. Achieving their goals should cost your characters something, too. Ask yourself: What will my hero/heroine need to give up in return for success?

By revealing the price to be paid, an author increases reader interest and tension. Will physical hardships, financial and other risks be worth the final payoff? Even if the character suffers horrendous hardships, will this guarantee his success?

One common difficulty with middles is the stagnant conflict or threat. In these novels, the conflict has been introduced near the beginning of the story and is a recurring theme, but it never seems to get any worse. The tension plateaus. Each instance of threat, each hurdle to be leaped seems a mirror image of previous incidents.

One of my students was writing a story about a woman who is frightened by a stalker. The character notices somebody following her on the street one day. Another day she is being followed again, this time as she boards the Metro. A third time she sees the same person in the grocery store. But these experiences remain at the same level of confusion or fear; there is no heightening of emotional intensity and no actual physical threat.

This author had to realize that she needed to raise the stakes and show an ever increasing upsurge of menace. Rewriting the middle of her story, she added the following incidents: 1) heroine observes stranger lurking outside her apartment when she gets home from work, 2) heroine thinks she recognizes the person and has uncomfortable but confusing memories, 3) heroine looks out apartment window and sees what looks like the same person trying to break into her car, 4) heroine finds a threatening and abusive note under her car's windshield wiper, 5) heroine becomes aware that someone has broken into her apartment; some of her clothing has gone missing, 6) heroine is grabbed from behind while walking in the park and forced into the woods. And so forth.

By making the situation darker, more urgent, harder for the character to deal with, no matter what genre you're writing, you will keep readers wondering *what happens next?*

### *Inject More Emotion*

One of the least understood but best tools available to any fiction author, anywhere in a story, happens to be the most difficult for many writers. That is: building emotion into the scenes. If this comes naturally for you, great. Emotion pumped up, realistically, just to the point of nearly being over the top, is a sure way to engage and hold readers.

If you have trouble putting emotion on the page, there are ways to learn.

Earlier in this book we discussed why emotion works so well to connect readers with characters: emotion is universal. Customs, religion, lifestyles, geography, and climate portrayed in a story may vary wildly from one tale to another. But all human beings (real or, I suspect, imaginary) feel emotion unless you create a world entirely populated by Mr. Spocks of *Star Trek* fame.

We can't assume readers will automatically "get" that a particular character is tormented by having lost a child, or will worry about starving, or feel overwhelming sadness at the loss of a loved one. We need to *show* the character in a frenzy, losing sleep, weeping, or expressing their emotions in some other physical, visual way.

As the author, you are already in tune with your characters and empathize with them. (At least, I hope you do.) But, generally, readers only know what you put on the page. You need to help them get in touch with your central characters' deepest feelings.

Think about what physical reactions you experience when you are scared, happy, angry, worried, or in love. Use that information to show your character reacting. Do you get anxiety headaches? Does your stomach hurt or do you have ulcers that act up when you are stressed? When frightened do you tremble or break out in tears? Depending upon your character's personality, or other traits and habits you've built into him, some of these reactions may be right on target. Or not realistic at all.

What about those times when we're in one character's head (aka Point of View) and we wish to show an emotional reaction from another person in the scene? Well, we can (through the POV character) observe the external effects of emotion on this other individual. From these physical clues, both the observing character and the reader will gather hints as to what that person is thinking or feeling. We interpret a frown, teary eye, or bared teeth in an attempt to better understand this human being.

In fact, your reader may interpret a character's external reactions entirely differently from the way characters do in the story. By leaving some reactions open to interpretation, we are able to let readers in on the game. We can either inform or, if we like, misinform the reader. Maybe the observed character is faking sadness by producing crocodile tears, but the POV character mistakenly sees this reaction as honest emotion. Meanwhile, your savvy reader suspects the sobbing teenager or less-than-contrite mourner is faking it!

Emotion is my Achilles' heel when it comes to my own writing. I dislike confrontation in real life. As a result I instinctively try to protect my characters from situations that might cause them pain. But I know if I don't allow my fictional people to face tough challenges and, sometimes, terrible danger, they won't be as interesting and may never achieve their full potential. And so, I always dive back into my story and work hard to intensify their emotional reactions. I make life a challenge for them. Then I enable them to show their feelings as they struggle to overcome whatever obstacles stand in the way of their happiness.

### *Show, Don't Tell Redux*

"Haven't we already been there, done that?" you ask.

Yes, we did indeed talk earlier in this book about the old axiom *Show, Don't Tell*. But, as with any complex and lengthy task, we get tired long before we reach the end of our labors. Writing a book demands a lot more of us physically and mentally than writing shorter fiction or articles. It's the difference between running a marathon and the one hundred-yard dash.

Both types of races are challenging and require similar skills. However, if you want to win an actual marathon, you can't stop to rest. You need to keep on running and not slow down. Thankfully when we're writing a book, we can slow down, regroup, take a morning or a day to refresh ourselves for the next leg of our journey. For many of us, that place to recharge our muse comes in the middle of the book.

Here is where we remind ourselves to return to the basics of creating scenes. What is a scene? Well, it has a beginning, a middle, and an end. A scene has at least one character, maybe more. It takes place in one setting but may segue into another location to follow a particular point-of-view character. We also need to provide visuals for the reader's benefit. Vivid details and a sense of motion. And, if possible, we should show the POV character interacting with one or more other characters through dialogue and action. All of which help build a movie in the reader's head.

Of course, these tips are already familiar to us. But sometimes, as we eagerly speed through our story, excited about finishing it (or worried about losing steam), we forget to do the jobs we did so well in the initial chapters of the book.

Instead, we slip into a habit of taking short cuts. While we're writing fast, (as I'm encouraging you to do), there's a tendency to write in less and less detail and end up in little more than synopsis mode. We resort to a sort of shorthand that fails to bring each scene into focus. If we recognize that this is merely a sketch of the action, and use it later to at least provide structure for a full revision—we've still done our job. But we absolutely *must* remember to finish the scene, fleshing out the bones with the missing action, details, characterization, dialogue, and emotion.

It's natural to fall back on our strongest skills when creating a rough first draft. We give ourselves permission to temporarily shelve those skills we haven't mastered quite as thoroughly. And that's all right. Eventually, though, we need to return and pick up the slack.

For instance, if our dialogue skills are a bit shaky, we might rely more heavily on narration or description to sketch a scene. We'll promise ourselves to give dialogue more attention in the later drafts. Generally, though, the more *showing* we do in our first draft, at least attempting to introduce a mixture of all the necessary elements—the less time we'll need to spend on future drafts. And that means a shorter overall time to completion, which is what most of us want.

If you discover that you've been developing scenes too thinly, even for a first draft, take a deep breath, ease up on that keyboard, and give yourself permission to reduce your daily page count just a smidge. The idea is to avoid a full lapse into synopsis humdrum.

Write the best you can, using your strongest techniques. Stress whatever skills you're most comfortable with, adding in other bits as you're able. No need to return to earlier sections of the story to make corrections to too-lightly sketched scenes. You'll know to hit those places harder when it comes time to revise.

Continue moving forward and showing each segment of your story as vividly as your imagination allows. Bring the reader ever closer to resolution of the conflict and the end of the story.

### Speaking of the end of the book...

The middle of any story is also a great time to tie up at least a few secondary plot threads. By resolving some issues that the characters have been struggling with (puzzles, mysteries, secrets, misunderstandings, whatever) before the actual end of the book, fewer explanations will be necessary in the closing moments of the story.

After all, isn't this a more likely way to conclude any experience? In real life, every challenge we face doesn't get resolved at the same time and tied up in a neat package, bow on top. In fact, leaving one or two minor issues in a character's life unresolved also mirrors life.

Many jobs await the author in the middle chapters of a novel. Now you'll know there's no reason to fear that once-barren no man's territory. We have, in fact, discovered *so much* work we can do that we may have to put a stop to adding more "stuff" and just move on to wrapping up the story.

So here we go—toward climax, resolution, and The End.

## Chapter 11: Satisfying Endings

Human nature longs for balance and justice. We can't always have that in the real world. We can in stories.

Readers trust an author to deliver a resolution to their novel that gives them an emotional payoff in the form of an ending that's satisfying in some way. To not give your reader that final positive experience before you say good-bye is bound to disappoint. This is the moment when your reader leans back in his chair as he closes your novel and thinks, *Ah, yes, that makes sense. That's how this must end.*

We don't need to supply the perfectly happy, everything's rosy, riding-off-into-the-sunset ending. But it must be logical in that the characters, plot, setting, and all that has transpired sufficiently support this particular resolution. It makes sense and gives the reader a final emotional takeaway. If we do it right, our readers will still be musing over those last dramatic scenes of the story hours or even days later.

Why do we owe our readers a reasonably believable and well-structured resolution? This is the reward for their having stuck with us through the entire book. They've surrendered precious time to participating in our art. They've opened their hearts and allowed themselves to become emotionally vulnerable while living vicariously with our characters and their dilemma. We *owe* them this.

Every once in a while, an author decides to ignore this responsibility by leaving the ending of their story hanging or obscure. We're not talking about those nifty kids' Choose-Your-Own-Ending adventure stories. Those can be fun. Providing multiple possible conclusions to a tale allows the reader to participate, which works particularly well with kids. But not so much for adult fiction.

Two adult novels that come to mind are Graham Greene's *Brighton Rock* and Mo Hayder's *Hanging Hill*. We simply have no firm resolution in either novel. Both are well-written books, but the release of tension that readers expect at the end of a story isn't there. It's enough to drive the poor reader mad!

Take the time to answer at least the most critical questions in your readers' minds. Wrap up the loose ends of your central plot. Give your audience a moment to enjoy that release of tension and sense of completion. Chances are, they'll go looking for other novels you've written. And if you've done your job particularly well, they'll be a fan for life.

### *Prepare, prepare, prepare*

Readers need to be made aware of various outcomes for a plot. If all the options seem potentially feasible, they will try to guess how things will turn out. Make your reader fear the worst, hope for the best, and feel the suspense building, until the glorious moment when all is resolved in a way that makes sense.

That isn't to say that the conclusion can't come as a surprise to the reader. (Possibly even to the author!) But because you've cleverly, subtly prepared them, revealing a collection of possibilities (e.g., the killer is disclosed and punished, the killer escapes to kill again, the killer dies in a dramatic final scene, the killer is found to be innocent), readers will be unsure until the final reveal. And, if you've done your job right, they'll recall the clues you planted earlier that support your chosen ending.

### Happy vs. Sad Endings

I'm always surprised by how many new writers decide, either before they start writing their story or during the process, that the ending of their novel must be a grim one in order to have any weight, any importance. They fully intend to leave their characters in misery, to one degree or another.

"It's just more realistic," some tell me. "Life is hard. There aren't many happy endings in the real world."

That may well be true. And you certainly can write a serious story in which not all of your characters come out well in the end. In fact a tale can be as dark as you like. Dark is good stuff in suspense stories, horror, thrillers, gothic tales, and moody literary works. But, with the possible exception of horror stories or dystopian adventures in which nearly everyone dies a bloody death (we presume *some* readers enjoy this), most book lovers find the truly downer ending disturbing and unwelcome.

Consider the classic tale *Charlotte's Web*, written by E. B. White. The story ends on a bittersweet note. The little pig mourns the loss of Charlotte the spider, his adored mentor and friend. But White was smart enough to leave the reader not with death in the forefront, but with a comforting thought. He gave us hope in the form of Charlotte's babies—the new generation— which Wilber the pig will now protect and raise.

It is this sense of hope for the future that makes the difference between a dejected reader, who can't understand why you killed off her favorite character at the end, and the reader who goes away encouraged: *Although life is harsh and eventually we all die, there is something to live for.* White's tale isn't just a children's story; it speaks to all of us.

Think about the many good stories you've read and most loved. Didn't each one have an ending that left you feeling completed, reflective, relieved, or renewed? As you consider possible endings for your novel, reflect on your options for sending readers away experiencing at least one of these emotions.

There is another reason for authors to choose resolutions that will please.

Very simply, happy endings are historically easier to sell than those that end in misery. After all, readers come to fiction for one reason more than any other. To be entertained. They want to escape into another (better?) life or place or time. They're happy to learn painlessly about any number of things—history, science, the law, horticulture, whatever—through the characters who act out the drama as you tell their story. But mostly they wish to experience the joy and newness of an adventure.

In particular, people who are bored with their everyday existence, who feel their lives have somehow gone wrong, who feel trapped in a world not of their liking—these folk long to escape into fiction. Some may even face serious health issues or other personal challenges. They come to our books to be distracted from the less than pleasant reality of their own lives. They come to dream along with us.

As authors we can't help them in their real lives, but we can give them a window into a new world, a new way of thinking, or a few hours of pleasure. That's an amazing gift to share with anyone.

In a less altruistic way, literary agents and editors of publishing houses also consider audience-pleasing elements in the novels they are reviewing. They know that bringing beloved characters to the brink of disaster, then letting them prevail over evil or a sad fate, provides a pleasurable jolt that readers long for. For these pros, it's always a matter of the bottom line—which means, how many copies of this book will sell and how much money the author's work will earn for their company.

### *The Reality of Publishing Today*

If we're serious about creating careers as novelists, we need to be realistic about the finances of publishing. What level of income does the average novelist actually earn in a year?

According to a September 2010 article in the *Wall Street Journal*, the remaining major publishers were offering contracts to debut novelists less frequently, leaving authors to turn to smaller regional or independent presses. The midsize to larger presses at that time were paying an average of $1,000 to $5,000 for advances against future earned royalties. But times have been hard on the publishing industry since then.

Today, many small and midsize presses pay no advance at all to their authors. In fact, some "hybrid" publishers expect the author to share in the expense of publishing their novel. Thus, even if an author writes two (or more) novels a year, the money handed over to the author on signing a contract (if any is offered at all) isn't enough to survive on. And there is no guarantee that the author will ever "earn out" his advance and then start receiving twice-a-year royalties on his books.

*The Guardian* newspaper (London) conducted a survey that disclosed the average income earned by the self-published authors they sampled in 2011 was $10,000. And, sure, we sometimes hear about outliers like Amanda Hocking with sales of $2.5 million, or Hugh Howey (the author of the science-fiction bestseller *Wool*) whose income no one really knows, but the survey found that at least half of all self-published authors made $500 or less annually.

More recently, in July of 2014, admitted data-geek Howey "pulled data for nearly every ranked ebook on Amazon.com's category bestseller lists" and passed along the emerging trends to assist authors in making decisions vital to their careers. (See it here: http://authorearnings.com/report/july-2014-author-earnings-report/ )

According to this report, author incomes from literary and children's fiction continued to be discouragingly low from all platforms (Big-Five, Small-Medium publishers, Indies) falling well beneath $50,000 and most clustering in the lower five-figures. However, Indie authors scored substantial incomes in the romance, science fiction/fantasy, and mystery/thriller/suspense genres. In fact, within the wildly varied romance category, Howie reported, 66 percent of independently published e-book authors sampled in his study earned just under $300,000, which is nothing to sneeze at.

*But these substantial payoffs are for books that not only fit into the above best-selling genres, they went into the bank accounts of authors whose books had already risen into major best-seller lists.* In short, these are figures that apply to the *success stories*, to authors who already have a large and enthusiastic following. Frequently these earnings reflect not one book, but a half dozen or many more by the same author.

Landing on the *New York Times* bestseller lists and drawing a six-figure income from a first novel does happen. But such instant success is comparable to winning the lottery. You can aim toward that goal and hope for the best, but don't count on it. It's wiser not to quit your day job yet. Know that it will take dedication and lots of hard work and time to get there, if it ever happens.

This isn't meant to discourage, just to put the publishing business in perspective.

### *It's a Business*

Earlier in this book, we spoke of compromise as we plan and execute our novels. Sometimes it makes sense to ask yourself:

*Do I need to write my story exactly as I first envisioned it?*

*Could your creative spirit see to making small but important changes within the general concept of your novel that might make it more interesting to a larger number of readers?*

The choice, as writers, is ours.

If no other genre except the traditional Western will suit you, even though very few Westerns are published each year, then you need to follow that vision. You may be the next Larry McMurtry.

But what if you decided you could be open to other possibilities? That same plot involving a gunslinger who saves a town from a dreadful pack of desperadoes might be tweaked to take place in outer space. Or you might write it as what's called a "time slip," in which characters from one time and place are somehow transported into an entirely different era. Either of those versions might attract a larger audience. Could you live with that new direction?

If you hadn't planned on writing a love story at all, but can see ways to involve a secondary plot line with a little romance—that change might give you more opportunities for publication.

If you are dead set on including a dozen exotic settings in your espionage novel, might you consider using just a couple and giving readers a more in-depth understanding of those locations—rather than making the book read like a travelogue? After all, those other settings can be saved for Books two, three, and four of your best-selling series.

Dig down for creative ways to nudge the plan for your novel in a direction that gives it more chances for catching a broad and enthusiastic readership. Chances are, you'll fall in love with these new ideas, just as you did with your original concept.

## Chapter 12: Revision & Next Steps

If you've stuck with me this far, congratulations. Have you been working on your novel as you were reading? Are you just starting, in the middle, or finishing it at this very moment? Wherever you are in the process, it's my hope you've picked up a few tips from this book to help you manage the more challenging tasks involved in getting your novel written.

Let's take a moment to summarize just a few points.

The goal of an Extreme Novelist is to quickly and aggressively rough-draft a book-length story suitable for publication. By writing fast and consistently, we are silencing The Voices that reduce our best intentions to author angst, and will ultimately keep us from succeeding, if we listen to them.

We are also letting our subconscious do more of the heavy lifting as we move through our draft. While we are writing, we are learning our story, discovering its shape, tone, and boundaries. We're also discovering how many characters are needed and something about each of them. We're exploring conflict, using fiction techniques to build tension and suspense, and finally seeking resolution. In short, we're building a resilient and logical structure for our novel by making many choices and constantly steering the story in a specific direction.

Once you've mastered these skills, you're well on your way to making your novel a reality. Although the writing will be far from polished (or publishable) at this point, you have established a workable, personal writing routine that will carry you through the revision process. Your ninety-minutes/day, six-days-a-week regimen (or whatever you set as your best pace) will have become a habit. A fiercely demanding habit that will be even harder to break than it was to form.

Many of my students report feeling emotionally distraught, angry, or frustrated when they are forced by external circumstances (i.e., the day job, family demands, illness) to set aside their writing for a time. And that's actually a *good* thing if you're a writer!

One of the magical benefits of intense daily writing is how deeply you will fall into your own story. You will be "living in the book" and may sometimes feel more intimately connected with your story than you do with your real life. You may hear your characters' voices in your sleep, imagine your paper people in all sorts of situations. You may wake in the middle of the night, compelled to jot down a fragment of dialogue or a new idea for a scene. And you most assuredly will discover many more options for your plot than if you wrote slowly and cautiously.

Does this sound a little crazy? Maybe to the nonwriter. But the human imagination feasts on this sort of fling-yourself-into-the-story writing. It repays the writer with increasingly juicier possibilities for the story and jolts of enthusiasm, even after a string of difficult writing days.

When you reach the final scene of your novel, you will probably take a long, hard look at your draft and think to yourself: *What a horrid mess!* And that's okay. Remember what we said at the outset of this adventure in writing an eight-week draft. *It's not going to be pretty.* But with every pass we make, with every stroke of the pen or deleted-and-replaced word on the screen, the manuscript will look cleaner, read stronger, feel more convincing, and come closer to publication quality.

Every writer possesses a personal set of writing skills that range from novice to professional. Revision will help you fine-tune all of them. In the next weeks and months you may shift the order of the story's events. Perhaps discard scenes or entire chapters, add in others. You might need another character. The emotional reactions of your characters may need elevation. You'll see places where you could have spiked the tension. The important thing is, you'll recognize these opportunities for making the book better, and then you can work on them.

Authors who allow themselves to appreciate the exhilaration and joy of writing like Extreme Novelists will love the process. Some of my students tell me they'll never go back to their old way of writing a first draft. But once you're ready to make revisions, you'll feel another kind of excitement. Now you get to switch hats, become the editor, and make your story sparkle and become truly readable and exciting. This is where you can unleash that perfectionist in you and search for the perfect word to reveal your vision of the story. Whereas when drafting a story we turned off the analytical and critical part of the brain...now we fully engage it.

Shouldn't we have been doing this all along? Shouldn't we have been writing to the very best of our ability from the beginning? Absolutely not. Remember what we said about expecting too much of ourselves? We've learned that we can't toggle that nonexistent switch in our brain and force it to jump back and forth between creative work and critical work.

The Voices may occasionally harass us, demanding that we do it all. It's hard to leave our prose in a less than perfect state. But if we write like the wind, we can outrun those negative messages.

This working draft is flawed. We can accept that. So exactly how do we revise to make it as amazing as we'd imagined it might be?

At the school where I teach we have courses on revising fiction for publication. This analytically based process requires an entirely different set of skills. That's probably why whole books have been written about revision techniques. We can't do justice to that new topic in a mere chapter at the end of this book. But if all goes well, *The Extreme Novelist Revises* will be available soon. This second book will focus on in-depth troubleshooting and the many ways to make a good story even better, bringing it up to publication quality.

For now, let's consider just one more often-expressed question.

### How do I know when I'm done?

By the end of the process of completing multiple drafts of a novel, we're tired. Moreover, we are incapable of determining whether or not changing a word here, a scene there will make any real difference. So there comes a time when we simply have to release our baby.

I think the best way of thinking about the done-ness of a book is something like this: *A novel is finished when the author has worked to the very best of her ability at this particular moment in her writing career.* That is, we know of nothing else to do.

Experienced writers agree that they are now writing far better than when they began their careers. Just as professional musicians progress in their skills as they practice, writers can expect to see their craft strengthen from one year to the next.

We are flexing our mental muscles, our writerly reflexes, our artistic instincts. The more we write, the stronger these muscles become. As long as we're cognizant of what our best writing is, and look to other talented writers to guide us and help us improve our skills, we will continue to grow. The more we learn, the faster our confidence in our ability to write good fiction will build.

But something even more magical happens to our writing from one month to the next. As we discussed earlier in this book, our writing changes as we ourselves change. Life comes at us, and our experiences grab us and throw us into the future where we scramble to survive and make sense of this new episode in our life. Five years from now, you will be a different person, and so will I.

Our writing will reflect our views, whether they are the same as they once were or have morphed into something entirely different. Our choices of words and topics for our fiction will reflect what we've learned and now care deeply about. We can expect to not only write better books in the future, but books born of deeper wisdom and insight. And that's a wonderful thing to look forward to.

In the meantime, what we write now will be good. Very good. And certainly not anything to be embarrassed by or ashamed of. This writing is uniquely ours, and we will allow our creative-self full rein to envision and put into words a story that we will eventually share with others.

What we are experiencing as working writers, as *Extreme Novelists*, is a little miracle. From a blank page or empty screen, we will create peopled worlds that others may delight in. There is, to my mind, no more satisfying art than this: Sharing a story with the world.

I wish you many happy writing hours and the joy of holding your very own book in your hands, as well as in your heart.

# THE EXTREME NOVELIST

## Dear Reader:

Thank you for choosing *The Extreme Novelist* as you explore the process of creating an amazing novel. I hope you now feel more confident as you continue your journey, writing book-length fiction that will appeal to readers everywhere. If you feel moved to do so, I'd be honored if you posted a review of this book on Goodreads.com, Amazon.com, or on your other favorite retail or review sites. Tips from this book that have smoothed your way through the writing process may prove equally valuable to other writers.

You may want to keep an eye out for other books in *The Extreme Novelist* series, available soon. These will include:
*The Extreme Novelist: A Workbook for the Time Deficient Author*
*The Extreme Novelist: Inspiration for the Twenty-First Century Author*

Meanwhile, I would love to hear from you. You can reach me here: Kathryn@WriteByYou.com. Or you may wish to stay in contact for additional tips and insights into the world of fiction and publishing by signing up for my monthly newsletter, *For the Love of Fiction*: http://eepurl.com/D8so9

If you live in the Washington, DC; Maryland; or Virginia area, check out my upcoming courses at The Writer's Center in Bethesda, Maryland (http://www.Writer.org). I'd be thrilled to see you in class. Throughout the year I offer inspiration to authors and others, speaking across the country at various writers' conferences and for organizations concerned with literacy and the arts. If we run into each other, please step up and introduce yourself. I want to hear all about your writing adventures!

Happy writing!
 Kathryn Johnson
www.WriteByYou.com
http://facebook.com/Kathryn.K.Johnson.3
Follow me on Twitter @KathrynKJohnson
Kathryn@WriteByYou.com

# KATHRYN JOHNSON

## Author's Bio:

Kathryn Johnson lives in Maryland with her husband and feline writing partners. Forty-three of her novels have been published by major U.S. and foreign publishers. She has written under her own name and a variety of pen names, including Mary Hart Perry, Kathryn Jensen, KM Kimball and Nicole Davidson. She teaches fiction-writing workshops for *The Writer's Center* in Bethesda, Maryland. Her popular 8-week course, *The Extreme Novelist*, supports and encourages class members through a full first draft of their novels. In 2008, she founded *Write by You*, a writer's mentoring service, to aid individual authors in reaching their publication goals. She has been nominated for the prestigious Agatha Christy Award, and won the Heart of Excellence and Bookseller's Best Awards. Her most recent novels include a trilogy of Victorian thrillers inspired by the lives of Queen Victoria's daughters (writing as Mary Hart Perry), and a new contemporary romantic-suspense series, *Affairs of State*. Current titles available: *Mercy Killing, Hot Mercy,* and *No Mercy*. Kathryn is a member of the Author's Guild, Romance Writers of America, Mystery Writers of America, Sisters in Crime, Novelists Inc, and the Historical Novel Society.

Made in the USA
Middletown, DE
04 January 2021

30681133R00085